Y0-BQN-965

THE AGED ARE PEOPLE, TOO

KENNIKAT PRESS

NATIONAL UNIVERSITY PUBLICATIONS

SERIES IN AMERICAN STUDIES

Under the General Editorial Supervision of

JAMES P. SHENTON

Professor of History, Columbia University

WILLIAM POSNER

April 28, 1913—April 16, 1961

THE AGED ARE PEOPLE, TOO

About
WILLIAM POSNER AND
SOCIAL WORK WITH THE OLD

by
MARY BUCKLEY

with an introduction by
ARTHUR S. FARBER

NATIONAL UNIVERSITY PUBLICATIONS
KENNIKAT PRESS
PORT WASHINGTON, N.Y./LONDON/1972

Library of Congress Catalog Card No.: 74-189553
ISBN: 0-8046-9024-3

Manufactured in the United States of America

Published by
Kennikat Press, Inc.
Port Washington, N.Y./London

To my husband Niel,

who likely would have greeted older days as he did his own last days—with a pleased and wondering,

"Well now, what have we here?"

CONTENTS

THE AGED ARE PEOPLE, TOO

Acknowledgments

So many persons through so many years have helped bring this book into being. For Arthur and all, my thanksgiving.

INTRODUCTION

I FIRST MET William Posner in the spring of 1951. Over the decade I knew him, my initial impression stayed with me and deepened. He was an unassuming, quiet, truly humble man, a genuine idealist and a person who practiced and lived what he believed in. And he believed in people, in all aspects of their being and their capacity for growth. This belief encompassed both those to be served and those who were there to help.

Those to be served in that "accident" of career choice for both of us happened to be older persons and their families. "Why do you want to work with the elderly?" he asked me on this first occasion of our meeting when we were discussing the possibilities of my joining with him in his work. I had no previous experience along this line. "Perhaps," I told him, "it was the good feeling I had about my relationship with my grandmother," and recalled nostalgically a time as a young boy when on a hot day she had greeted me lovingly with a kiss on the cheek and a large white cup of very cold milk and a fresh, buttered Kaiser roll. "Oh, how good that had been for you," Posner replied and then reminisced about his too having been loved by his grandparents. He wished that more families could "be willingly tied but need not be unwillingly bound." His professional life was dedicated, among other things, to this generational goal.

Posner did not mean that in order to work with the aged

3

one must have loved or been loved by his grandparents, or
for that matter be young or old, or a beginning or seasoned
worker in one's professional development. But whatever it
was that the helper brought, Posner looked for that spark
of interest and that potential which might respond with enthusiasm and caring to this work, and in fact he attracted
around him and nurtured a coterie of such people both on
his staff and in his widespread contacts with others.

Each of us who reads and studies this book will be in-
debted to its author, for she has most ably performed a
Boswellian task. Mary Buckley did not know Posner, yet
she has written about him as if she really did. In true
ecumenical spirit Mrs. Buckley, a devout Episcopalian, who
happens to be the Director of Social Service of a Catholic
home for the aged, writes this professional biography about
Posner, who was an observant Orthodox Jew. Thus, there
is this spiritual bond. But what Posner and his professional
biographer have in common transcends their deep, living
religiousness, which, incidentally, was not obvious to many,
certainly never imposed. Both subscribed to practicing, in
humanistic ways, their beliefs about working with and helping people. Humility, a sense of purpose, responsibleness,
and the capacity for scholarly, hard work were also shared
temperamental characteristics. Mrs. Buckley's success in
this book, then, comes out of a deep affinity in philosophy
and outlook between herself and her subject.

How does Posner's work fit into a larger framework that
deals with previous work with the aged? What was his place
in the history of social work with older people? What are
the implications of his contribution? What were his lasting
achievements?

A bench mark scholarly article which Mrs. Buckley
writes about (see pp. 102-107) was Posner's 1958 Council
on Social Work Education Aspen Conference paper in
which he reviewed the previous forty years of writing about
casework with the aged. No one had done this before nor
has anyone since. This look at history in itself was a decided

contribution to the field for it gave perspective, was a summing up, and set the course for the next period ahead.

During the 15 years following World War II, work with the elderly was devalued as unrewarding and professionally unstimulating, yet Posner turned this nihilism into its opposite. He became a gerontological advocate. His work presaged things to come and he left a number of notable contributions that are useful today and promise to be enduring. Mary Buckley's book on Posner and his writings on social work with the aging brings together the central ideas of about fifty of his written papers. This assemblage and distillation of what he had to say is a treasure for those interested in services to the elderly in terms of its historical value, early theory-building formulations and enduring practice-based wisdom.

It has been said that "Our professional history suggests that often practice in fact precedes theory-building. The pragmatic or useful leads us on, while the theoretical rationale is formulated later. Ideally, practice and theory should be partners. In reality there are time lags: What we do and what we say we do are often at variance." (34) Posner had a way of being in touch with a practice that was in advance, and he conceptualized the practice he knew in order to promote theory.

What were William Posner's contributions? What developments have taken place since the 1961 White House Conference year in which he died? What are the continuities of his contributions in relation to changing developments? Mrs. Buckley's book answers a good part of such questions regarding the man's contributions. The following will perhaps highlight the most notable and lasting of these while also commenting on subsequent developments and trends since Posner's death.

The heart of Posner's creative contribution to practice, perhaps, is to be found in his development of the adult private residence program. Under his direction, as described in the 1965 Encyclopedia of Social Work(28), it was one

of the first private agency programs in foster home placement of older persons. He shaped adult foster home placement into a sophisticated service that met individualized
human needs—needs of the older person, needs of adult
children or other family members, and the needs of the
foster family caretakers. Much of what Posner spoke about
on other broadened subjects was rooted in this practice experience from his agency. For his article about this specially
crafted service, he received honorable mention from the
Virginia P. Robinson Award in the spring of 1952 (see
Appendix C). Some readers, before getting into the chro-
nology of this book, may find it profitable to go directly to
this paper for a living-process, back-and-forth example of
the practice he developed and drew upon. Others may wish
to turn to the Robinson Award paper after reaching Mary
Buckley's description of the private residence service in the
text.

The adult foster home program was a viable, vibrant
example of one of a whole range of supports for living in the
community. Mrs. Buckley describes some of the other
support services such as homemaker service, housekeeping
service, counseling and volunteer service, all with a recur-
rent theme of offering client-centered, need-focused help.

These social supports for being able to stay in one's own
or substitute home have euphemistically been called alternatives to institutional care as if the real or expected solution was placement in an institution. This is too bad, but it
is the way social policy has thus far been developed in our
country. Actually, institutional care should really have
provided *an* alternative rather than *the* alternative to difficulties in being able to manage independently.

Posner was not against placement in institutions. He
applauded and promoted high standards in nursing homes
and homes for the aged, but warned against the dangers of a
"brick and mortar" psychology. In short, he believed in the
preeminence of community living and espoused the promotion of a whole range of socially supported programs to en-

able older people to live in the community. His pioneer work and development of the private residence program for adults, as one example of community based services, stands as a lasting and continuing contribution.

Among Posner's contributions was his "premature" identification of the significance of the cultural dimension in casework with the aged. At a time in the 1950s when assimilation was the mode and when it was unpopular to do so, he was "beyond the melting pot."(19) He encouraged efforts to understand cultural factors and to sensitively apply these insights in practice with people.

Mary Buckley's sound assessment (page 130) of Posner's "affirmation of difference" in regard to Jewishness and her comparison with the Black experience in the 1960s makes what he wrote on this topic contemporary and predictably modern for a long time to come. It will be interesting for the student of gerontology to note that analogous to the work that has been done on this general subject by Billingsly (2) and Rainwater(33), research in the field of aging of Black individuals and families has begun to be addressed by the Gerontological Society, particularly in the work of Jacquelyne Jackson.(22) (23)

Closely allied to this cultural dimension was Posner's coinage of the phrase the "generational component" as a key to the examination of intergenerational relations. Posner intuitively discarded the myths about the so-called self-sufficient nuclear family and the inevitable alienation of the generations. His was a foreview of what the unfolding theory and the research of the 1960s subsequently confirmed in such exciting work as that of Blenkner(4), Leichter and Mitchell(27), Schorr(39), and Shanas and Streib, et al.(41)

While Posner was a philosophical generalist about social work practice, he saw that this approach was simply not working in helping the elderly. Thus, he became a pragmatic specialist. Up to this point the generic approach failed to contribute to knowledge building and practice development. Since Posner was aware of the dangers of narrowness and confinement, the meaning of specialization for him was not segregation but rather relatedness to the needs of others within the social situation. Mary Buckley rightly calls Posner's use of specialization today's principle of concentration, and I might add that this was effectively enunciated in the revised 1970 curriculum statement of the Council on Social Work Education.(16)

His views about specialization are congruent with what has only recently come into clearer focus in social work in the thinking of Briar(8), Maas(29), and Turner(45), and now appears to be on the map for the 1970s in social work education and practice.

William Posner was en route to teaching in graduate social work education when he died, and had he lived, he would have been very much aware of and part of the continuities and the trends that emerged in the 1960s and 1970s. There are several developments that might have heartened him in his quest for more progress.

First, his hope that more research and study would unfold some answers or at least provide new directions was met in the late 1960s by an exciting proliferation of research reflecting a broadened scope and encompassing many disciplines.(46) A key series of three volumes, the first of which is an inventory edited by Riley and Foner(35), set a framework for research in aging and monitored what was being done. A notable example of cross-cultural study in three industrial societies was published in the works of Shanas with her associates.(40) Also worth referring to is the activity of the Gerontological Society who were commissioned to evaluate the state of research in the following areas: I. Work, Leisure, and Education; II. Living Arrangements of Older People: Ecology; III. Social Services for the Aged and Aging: Suggested Research Priorities; IV. Economics of Aging, and a subsequently published section on minorities and aging.(20) In addition, progress has been made in assessing the functioning of older persons.(21)

Major multidisciplinary gerontological centers with research and teaching foci have been developed in several university-based locations. Dr. Wilma Donahue gave leadership to what is perhaps the oldest center, now called the Institute of Gerontology, The University of Michigan—Wayne State University. The Center for the Study of Aging and Human Development founded by Dr. Ewald W. Busse was established at Duke University in North Carolina, and the Gerontology Center at the University of Southern California is under the direction of Dr. James Birren. There is also an Oregon Center for Gerontology at the University of Oregon with Dr. Francis Scott in charge. Dr. Clark Tibbitts of the Administration on Aging, a long-time gerontology advocate, is hopeful that in the 1970s there may be one such center established in each of the ten regions of the country.

In social welfare itself, research about the elderly has come from two major sources: (a) universities with doctoral programs in social work have produced an increasing volume of dissertations on this subject. Particularly notable in the field of aging have been the concentrations offered in social policy analysis, planning and administration at the Levinson Gerontological Policy Institute, Brandeis University. Each September the Social Service Review(43) publishes abstracts of completed doctoral dissertations where a fair idea can be obtained about the content dealt with and the range of themes covered; (b) a number of agency research centers have brought together top-flight research teams who have produced some significant research. Two such community-based centers are the Institute of Welfare Research of the Community Service Society of New York(5) and the Benjamin Rose Institute of Cleveland.(6) The Philadelphia Geriatric Center(21) and the Mansfield Memorial Homes of Mansfield, Ohio, have been attached to institutional complexes.

Second, in the context of his study of the last stages of the full life cycle, Posner became aware of the resistance and fears around death and dying. He dealt with the task of

seeing death as a natural part of life. Again, in the last five
years, there has been an amazing breakthrough of popular
interest, scientific study, and knowledge about death. Readers of a psychology magazine felt that death was apparently
more important than sex: there were 30,000 questionnaire
responses for the former subject contrasted with 20,000 for
sex.(42) New journals have sprung up(24)(38), and many
bibliographies developed attempting to keep up with the
tremendous production of books and articles. No bibliography is as yet all-encompassing, but the one by Vernick(47)
is reasonably current. Kubler-Ross' book(25), an outgrowth
of an interdisciplinary seminar she gave, is no doubt the
single, most comprehensive and significant work on this
topic. Dr. Ross' views are a must for anyone who is in the
helping role with the dying person and members of his
family.

Third, Posner asked significant and necessary questions
about the meaning of sex to the older person, again push-
ing past fears or embarrassment about what was still another taboo area. The Brechers'(7) popularization of the
work of Masters and Johnson(30) showed that about one-
third of the subjects in their studies of sexuality were older
persons. When one also draws upon the work of Rubin(37),
it becomes clear that there now is considerable new information available to replace the folk tales of the past.

Fourth, Posner saw an intimate relationship between
social work education and practice. He repeatedly goaded
the educational enterprise and established agencies for their
slowness in building knowledge and in contributing to
practice with the aged. As Mrs. Buckley points out, while
in the '60s some progress could be noted, Posner no doubt
would have considered it insufficient. However, a number
of developments might have pleased him. What were some
of the high points in practice and in education in these past
ten years?

It was the work of Wasser(49) based upon the four-year,
Ford Foundation–funded, Family Service Association of
America Project on Aging training experience with forty

voluntary private family agencies in the early 1960s that made the most notable contribution in casework with the aging. Wasser assembled and made available a circumspect and conceptualized presentation on the state of direct-service, practice knowledge with the aging, and also accompanying case illustrations.(48) Other important additions by social workers to the literature in this field have been made by Blenkner(3)(4), Brody(10)(11)(12)(44), and Pincus(31)(32), who have further delved into developmental theory, the dynamics of reminiscence and the life review, the nature of kinship, filial and family relations, and among other things what is involved in the provision of direct social service with the aged and their families, and the area of protective services for the older person.(6)(13)(21)(26)

A follow-up to the Council on Social Work Education, National Council on Aging, co-sponsored institute at Aspen, Colorado, held in 1958 was the 1966 Allerton House Conference in Illinois. The Aspen Conference produced two pamphlets.(17) About a third of the accredited schools of social work were represented at the 1966 conference and the levels of workshop participation indicated that some limited curriculum progress had been made particularly in the Human Behavior and Social Environment Sequence.

The National Institute of Mental Health has played a significant part in funding field work student units in direct services, as the Administration on Aging in parallel fashion has made possible the development of graduate school training, including field placements in community organization and administration.(18)

At the outset I mentioned the beginning of my working relationship with Posner. He had a profound effect on my life and the subsequent professional decisions which I made. My move into teaching was not unrelated to my awareness that this was what William Posner had been planning to do. It was not accidental that I chose to create a course on Adulthood in the Human Growth and Behavior sequence at the University of Washington School of Social Work and went on to direct a model project in aging involving students, faculty and community agencies serving older persons.

Fifth, Posner's was a unifying philosophy in that he not only perceived the individual and interpersonal dynamics but also stressed the connection with social factors. He constantly decried society's shortcomings in not assuring basic necessities such as income, health care, housing opportunities for education and social participation. He worked with other social welfare groups such as the New York City Health and Welfare Council on a local level and with the National Council on Aging, nationally, in order to spur understanding and social change on behalf of older persons.

Posner was actively involved in the 1961 White House Conference on Aging that contributed to the effort to document the needs of the aging and set out desirable goals. The limitation in the Conference was that there was a proliferation of program recommendations but relatively little in the way of clear policy proposals based on what Briar(9) calls sophisticated research and sound policy analysis.

Pre-planning for the 1971 White House Conference is focused on formulating a limited number of policy proposals on a range of basic needs and needs-meeting mechanisms that may be feasibly adopted—after widespread public debate and subsequent social and legislative action.(51) Illustrative of one of the high priority issues for the '70s is that of income highlighted in a background paper by Chen.(15)

What the 1961 White House Conference did accomplish was to demonstrate the potential of social advocacy for and with the aging illustrated by the movement for health care legislation. It uncovered the tremendous unmet health needs of the aged, gathered and assessed the requisite facts and provided the opportunity for the aged to be mobilized in alliance with their middle-aged, adult children and other interest groups in aging, all of which led to the passage of the Medicare legislation of the mid-1960s.

What that indicates, perhaps, is T. L. Peacock's contention that a single success shows that it can be done. Will the ideas of the social planners of the 1960s for maximum

17. Council on Social Work Education. *Social Work Education for Better Services for the Aging.* New York, 1959 and *Toward Better Understanding of the Aging.* New York, 1959.

18. *The Gerontologist* 10, nos. 2 and 3 (Spring and Summer 1970).

19. Glazer, Nathan and Daniel P. Moynihan. *Beyond the Melting Pot.* Cambridge, Mass.: The M.I.T. Press and Harvard University Press, 1963.

20. Havighurst, Robert J. "Research and Development Goals in Social Gerontology." Status Report. *The Gerontologist* 9, no. 4, pt. II (Winter, 1969). "Research Proposals in Applied Social Gerontology." Second Report 1971. *The Gerontologist* 11, no. 1, pt. II (Spring, 1971).

21. Howell, *et al.,* "A Symposium on the Assessment of Functions of the Aging Adult." *The Gerontologist* 10, no. 1, pt. I (Spring, 1970): 5–52.

22. Jackson, Jacquelyne Johnson. "Aged Negroes: Their Cultural Departures from Statistical Stereotypes and Rural-Urban Differences." *The Gerontologist* 10, no. 2 (Summer, 1970).

23. Jackson, Jacquelyne Johnson. "Social Gerontology and the Negro: A Review." *The Gerontologist* 7, no. 3, pt. I (September, 1967).

24. Kalish, Richard A., ed. *Omega* (an international journal for the psychological study of dying, death, bereavement, suicide and other lethal behaviors). Westport, Conn.: Greenwood Periodicals.

25. Kubler-Ross, Dr. Elisabeth. *On Death and Dying.* New York: Macmillan, 1969.

26. Lehmann, Virginia and Geneva Mathiasen. *Guardianship and Protective Services for Older Persons.* New York: National Council on Aging, 1963.

27. Leichter, Hope and William Mitchell. *Kinship and Casework.* New York: Russell Sage Foundation, 1967.

28. Lurie, Harry L., ed. *Encyclopedia of Social Work.* Fifteenth Issue, New York: National Association of Social Workers, 1965.

29. Maas, Henry, "Purpose, Participation and Education." In *Innovations in Teaching Social Work Practice.* Council on Social Work Education, 1970, pp. 11–15.

30. Masters, William H., M.D., and Virginia E. Johnson. *Human Sexual Response.* St. Louis, Missouri: The Reproductive Biology Research Foundation. Boston: Little, Brown and Co., 1966.

31. Pincus, Allen. "Reminiscence in Aging and Its Implications for Social Work Practice." *Social Work* 15, no. 3 (July, 1970).

32. Pincus, Allen. "Toward a Developmental View of Aging for Social Work." *Social Work* (July, 1967).

33. Rainwater, Lee. "Crucible of Identity: The Negro Lower-Class Family." *Daedelus, Journal of the American Academy of Arts and Sciences* (Winter, 1966), pp. 172–216.

34. Rapoport, Lydia. "Crisis-Oriented Short-Term Casework." *The Social Service Review* 41, no. 1 (March, 1967).

35. Riley, Matilda White and Anne Foner, eds. *Aging and Society I: An Inventory of Research Findings.* New York: Russell Sage Foundation, 1968–1969.

36. Riley, Matilda White, John W. Riley, Jr. and Marilyn E. Johnson. *Aging and Society* II: Aging and the Professions. New York, Russell Sage Foundation, 1969.

37. Rubin, Isadore, M.D. *Sexual Life After Sixty.* New York: The New American Library, Signet, 1967.

38. Schoenberg, Bernard, ed. *Archives of the Foundation of Thanatology.* New York: Foundation of Thanatology.

39. Schorr, Alvin. *Filial Responsibility in the Modern American Family.* Washington, D.C.: U.S. Dept. of Health, Education and Welfare, 1960.

40. Shanas, Ethel and associates. *Old People in Three Industrial Societies.* New York: Atherton Press, 1968.

41. Shanas, Ethel and Gordon Streib, eds. *Social Structure and the Family: Generational Relations.* Englewood Cliffs, N.J.: Prentice-Hall, 1965.

42. Shneidman, Edwin S. "You and Death." *Psychology Today* (June 1971), pp. 43–45, 74–80.

43. *The Social Service Review.* Chicago, Ill.: The University of Chicago Press. (A quarterly devoted to the scientific and professional interests of social work.)

44. Spark, Geraldine M. and Elaine M. Brody. "The Aged Are Family Members." Presented at the Conference on *Family Therapy and the Family Life Cycle,* Family Institute of Philadelphia, Pa., May 23, 1969, revised. Mimeographed.

45. Turner, John B. "In Response to Change: Social Work at the Crossroad." *Social Work* 13, no. 3 (July, 1968).

46. U.S. Dept. of Health, Education, and Welfare. *Adult Developments and Aging Abstracts.* Public Health Service, National Institute of Health.

47. Vernick, Joel J. *Selected Bibliography on Death and Dying.* Bethesda, Md.: National Institute of Child Health and Human Development, 1969.

48. Wasser, Edna L. *Casebook on Work with the Aging.* New York: Family Service Association of America, 1966.

49. Wasser, Edna L. *Creative Approaches in Casework with the Aging.* New York: Family Service Association of America, 1966.

50. Wasser, Edna L. *Selected Bibliography for Casework with Older Persons.* New York: Family Service Association of America, 1963.

51. White House Conference on Aging. *Technical Guide for Community and State White House Conferences on Aging.* Washington, D.C. (November, 1970).

"GIVINGLY"

..... about the man William Posner

WILLIAM POSNER USED the word "givingly" in describing how to serve a meal to older people living in other people's homes. It may have been a grammatical slip or a purposeful creation. No matter, it still remains a key word for telling about how William Posner hoped the aged would be received and helped, and for telling about what kind of man he was.

At one time he gave credit to the small number of dedicated social workers who had given of themselves and of their very being to draw attention to the possibilities for growth in older persons. For 12 years William Posner was one of these, giving of himself and his very being. Beginning with a basic conviction in the dignity of man as fundamental to our American way of life, he saw a failure in application where older people were concerned. He saw that there had been lip service only in according the dignity of either age or personhood to the aged person. As a social worker, he wanted social workers to lead the way in emphasizing worth and growth regardless of age, but he knew that this could hardly be done "unless we ourselves reevaluate our own attitudes and feelings toward the aged and develop the conviction that the aged are people, too."[1]

With a faith that all life is precious and each life is to be treasured, he gave of himself in a crusade dedicated to the goal that more might see the goodness and richness and development of later years, that they might see the ending

17

part of life as a time of fulfillment, a time to be anticipated, and that social work and society might bring back a respect and reverence for the aged years and the aged person.

A man of compassion, he saw and ached for those who found their last years to be years of loneliness and poverty and neglect, but refused to believe there was not a way up and out or that any life must be held hopeless. His faith in man's potential was founded firmly in faith in God. He saw social work as a profession that had limitless possibilities for contributing to the welfare of individuals and one that called for a positive and constructive involvement of self for man.

William Posner answered that call and givingly offered himself.

This book is not intended to be biographical but to bring together and set forth the many contributions of this man William Posner to the field of social work with the aged. A chronological outline of the major events of his life is available in Appendix A, but a few background facts are pertinent, with thanks to the friends who knew him then. By the time he was a senior in high school, he listed his hobby as "studying," and stated that his ambition was to be of service to humanity. The pattern of his life was already defined as he was to become a lifelong student and a selfless servant of humanity.

Having shown a distinct preference for the humanistic in college, Posner went on to the Pennsylvania School of Social Work in 1935. After a second-year fellowship with a foster home care agency, Posner stayed on as a full time worker and began twelve years of working, in Pennsylvania and New York, with foster children. Posner was a sick man during those years, but except for one serious operation, no one would have known this as his good feelings, friendliness, and giving attitudes were always present.

The final focus in his work began in 1948. By this time he was a District Supervisor for the Jewish Child Care Association of New York, but in the meantime, the Jewish

sis and his hard working quality "catching." Aptekar finds
it interesting that a number of the people he worked with
turned out to be like him in these respects, and that they
regard his work as invaluable. Although the field has moved
a great deal since his death they feel that what he accomplished has endured.

No, William Posner and I never met, but in the research
for this book, with the purpose of gathering in one package
a distillation of all he said in the nearly 40 articles available out of over 50 that he wrote, there came a sense of
knowing him well. The dedication to the aged comes through
throughout, with the frustration at the blindness of others
and at the ineffective superficiality of those who claimed
to care. Above all shines the humility of a man always
eager to learn, to achieve a deeper understanding, to search
the work of others and the depth of his own soul for the
sake of the older client.

There was a good deal of repetition in what he said and
wrote, for he took his cause to a broad audience, but in
reading his articles and speeches chronologically there is
an undeniable impression of the growth and development
of a social worker and of a man. The early articles somehow indicate the kind of person who would do a good and
thorough job of anything assigned to him. And the aged
were his assignment. But as the years go on and his involvement becomes wholly dedicated, the tone of responsibility
and commitment increases.

For instance, as he reviewed a decade of action in 1952,
it was just that—an enumeration of accomplishments. Several years later, he again reviews the recent past for the
1960 Seminar on Casework with Older People, and con-
fesses a struggle in the writing because of a compelling
sense of responsibility to formulate a statement that would
serve as meaningful and helpful background material. As
he continues, the recitation of facts is combined with an
urgent plea for more attention. His plea was for a serious,
forthright, and courageous attack on attitudes, an attack

that would mean a new level of self-revelation. The goal—
personal growth of the helpers for better help to the helped.

This awareness of the possibilities of growth for the
worker increases. Early he mentioned the mutual benefits
to be gained in working with older people. It seems obvious
that his own experience later led him to refer with such
conviction to the great importance of casework with the
aged not only as a unique helping process for the growing
numbers of aged but as a dynamic learning and growth
experience for those working with them, a point few seem
to have noticed then or notice now.

His frustration and impatience are somewhat revealed in
the articles, but there his aim was always to encourage a
forward thrust. The depth of his own personal distress was
expressed only privately as in letters to friend and one-time
fellow worker, Arthur S. Farber: "Where is the social work
mission? Where are our concerns for all people? Workers
today want to sit in their offices and do 'counseling'. The
challenge of the hard-to-reach client does not faze them."

And later: "At a certain point spreading the word for
the aged becomes a personal mission to which we've got to
respond." Respond he did. Social work and many an older
individual have been and will be enriched by his unqualified
response.

This has been something of the man William Posner.
Now to what the man said and did:

> We all know that as much as we might be concerned
> about a reality situation, it is the psychological or *atti-
> tudinal* component that leads us first to an *understanding*
> of it, then to its *acceptance* as important and valid for
> us, and finally to *action*.[5]

The italics are mine. The italicized words become the
framework to follow.

Notes

1. William Posner, "New Horizons in Casework with the Aged," Institute of Welfare & Health Council of New York City (March 1955), p. 16.
2. Louis Bernstein, "A Rabbi's Tribute," *William Posner: Memorial Journal,* Young Israel of Windsor Park (New York, 1963).
3. Maurice Hexter, "A Professional's Professional," ibid.
4. Sarah Tederman, "My Teacher," ibid.
5. William Posner, "Casework with the Aged as a Specialized Service in a Multiple Service Agency," paper presented for Jewish Community Services of Long Island (October 1952), p. 1.

"A PSYCHOLOGICAL BLOCK"

. . . . . about attitudes and values

ATTITUDE TO UNDERSTANDING to acceptance to action. Posner looked clearly at the situation as it was, then he began with the source of the situation—the attitudes of our society and ourselves toward older people. Nor was it enough to begin there. Over and over throughout his writings, he returned to the beginning, having seen advance in understanding and action but never enough to please him in that foundation of attitudes, or in a real acceptance of the validity of a new look.

That foundation of our society's attitudes, Posner found rooted in a firmly entrenched, almost impregnable stereotype that had developed in thinking about the aged. Perhaps it came from a slight understanding accepted as fact, from a building up of little bits and pieces at the expense of the whole of what older people are like. Perhaps it grew from making of false generalizations from specific personal experiences. Perhaps from the prejudices around us. Whatever, he found:

> The average person thinks of the aged man or woman as one who has outlived his usefulness and hence is unable to be productive and creative. He thinks of him as one who is unable to learn—best expressed in the proverbial expression "You can't teach old dogs new tricks." He does not believe the older person can change or make new adjustments. He thinks of him as one who is largely

dependent and unable very often to take on independence.[1]

That was in 1952. In 1960 he said much the same but with
that deepening of tone that was apparent in all the progression of his thought:

> Older years are seen less as years of maturity and
> wisdom than of loneliness and boredom. They tend to be
> looked upon as a time of loss—loss of friends and rela-
> tives, and loss of self-worth and self-esteem. . . . Present-
> day society. . . . has equated all aging with illness, loss
> of functions, and loss of skills. It has tended to categorize
> elderly people instead of individualizing them as is done
> with those of other age groups. There is, therefore, a
> tendency to believe that most older people are ill, or all
> older individuals lack speed and efficiency, or all elderly
> persons cannot fend for themselves.[2]

impat.

These are but two samples of the line of thought that
entered every article, every speech; and in each, by word
or implication, he went beyond the negative to stress the
positive. Our stereotypes are dangerous, our assumptions
are unfounded. This he began saying in his first article of
1949 after the experience of one year in a private residence
program. He had found in this one year sure evidence that
older persons *can* change and grow, that they *can* take responsibility for their living, that dynamic living does not
stop at age 60, but goes on even as life itself goes on.

Part of the difficulty on attitude came from a narrow and
negative view of thinking of aging and old age as a problem
rather than a normal part of the life process. The increased
possibility of chronic illness as our bodies age does not mean
we should think of all aging in pathological terms. But to
see it so, Posner saw as the temper of his time. He tried to
turn the view toward growth, certain that for most people
older years can be years of enrichment, years of accomplishment and creative activity. To him, aging was development,
progressing from one phase of life to another.

When he began his caring, Posner was almost alone in his conviction about the possibilities of growth in this last phase; at least, from the journals of the time, it seems not a thought worth mentioning. Age itself was so rarely mentioned. So at the ending of his career he found particular gratification in the uniqueness of the 1961 White House Conference on Aging because it went beyond the problems and presented for all to see the opportunities of older years as well. It was with pleasure that he noted that the Conference occupied itself not with the negative realities of aging but with the positive realities as well; not merely with the losses and declines that occur as we grow older, but also with the maturity, wisdom, and growth that exist as potentials for the great majority of older citizens; not merely with the fears of aging but with the blessings as well.

If continued development can be the norm for older people, where then are the stumbling blocks between possibility and a more common fulfillment? At first Posner simply accepted and stated the facts and the effect of being shunned and rejected by society. From the emotional standpoint, the fears and frustrations of an older person came partly from physical deterioration but even more from the impact of the attitude directed toward him. We of any age so often see ourselves as we believe others see us. Sometimes we judge what they think by what they do. So with the aged: growing mandatory retirement; refusal of employment to older persons as a general pattern in our society; the resultant economic dependence either upon public assistance or relatives; the shortage of suitable recreational, medical and social facilities for older persons; most of all the attitude that says "your opinion is outdated—you don't matter." Or "your presence is embarrassing—you're not wanted."

For those who stopped to consider, it began to be apparent that the emotional problems of older persons were not inherent in their years but related rather, as with other people, to the frustrations and insecurities created by the attitudes of others. Facing such a mirror without counteracting support, ability to use real inner strengths and capacities at least temporarily fails.

But by 1953 Posner was exploring the "why" of it, looking at the history behind the rejections. He found attitudes based largely upon cultural traditions and felt that unless we were ready to examine those traditions they would continue to lead to packaged thinking. Concern for the aged may have been a time-honored tradition, but the ways and methods of caring for them had been based upon these stereotyped attitudes—attitudes which came down to us from generation to generation.

What are some of these attitudes? Most of us will recognize them: older people are largely dependent and hence cannot fend for themselves; they are unable to assume independence; they cannot be creative; they are sick people and hence cannot participate in the normal day to day activities of most other people; they lack emotional stability due to the gradual deterioration that takes place in old age; older persons do not know what is good for them—they cannot choose between one thing and another; they cannot assume responsibility, hence others have to do it for them. There are so many other stereotypes that one can mention. What this adds up to is that we have isolated out the older person from the population as a whole. We have differentiated him so much from the rest of the community that the only method of care we could see for him was that type of care which would give him utmost protection. Hence the development of the institution. ... .[3]

He found the lack of recognition of the place of the older person in our society basic to the whole problem of attitudes. With our emphasis on youth, we had defined no role for the aged, something that Posner recognized a decade before it was generally accepted as essential to all persons. The changes of industrialization, the increased pace of living, the smaller units of housing all added to the development of the aged into a minority group. And underneath all the rejection he found our fear of the older person in our fear of our own future, our own aging and death.

In 1958 Posner did the first of several scholarly articles, in this one especially reviewing the history of the field. Here it was that he seemed heartened to find he was not alone, and that much he had believed was supported by these others. The progress of change in attitudes was described through the action developed more than in specific words, but Posner noted an article in 1922 that told of the feelings of shame and hate children of immigrants felt for their parents when they, the children, were trying to take on American ways.[4] He found in his search confirmation of his own impression of the general cultural attitude—"shelve the older person."

However, both the background and effect of society's shunning and shelving are expressed most persuasively in the manual on policies and procedures prepared by Posner and Mrs. Rochelle Indelman for the staff in services for the aged of the Long Island agency.

Our culture, so much influenced by socio-economic factors, conditions us to believe that the older person is not interested in, or entitled to, the same opportunities for growth and satisfaction as the younger one. The resulting deprivations bring about emotional and psychological changes in his self-esteem and self-worth. His sense of usefulness is diminished; he is forced to retire gradually into a more limited way of living; his zest and physical vigor are no longer stimulated; his will loses its independence. Such a person begins to be considered by his environment as "old." To a great extent society itself produces the problems of "old age," but does little to prevent them.

Our present-day culture, which evolves around tremendous new technological devices, rejects the person who has difficulty in accepting the new tempo or method of living. The younger person follows it more easily. It brings about great psychological gulfs between the young and the old without much consideration for the contributions the older person made to bring about the changes.*

Hence, the older person finds himself excluded from the activities of younger people and often is made to feel inferior. Again here, no provision is made to sustain the older person's interests.

The paradox in medical progress demonstrates this best. Serious effort is being made through research to prolong human life and to reduce human physical suffering. But little parallel effort is made to sustain and maintain useful life. Nothing is spared to keep a person alive as long as possible, but little is done to make it a satisfactory and productive life.[5]

There is an element of emotion in these teaching words, a depth of feeling that is more apparent when Posner is speaking to his own staff, his own profession, than when he is addressing society as a whole. For it is here in his own profession that he beseeches us to look clearly into our own hearts for our own attitudes and values, not only as expressed by our words, but also as shown by our actions.

His plea began in 1948 when he shared the effect of specialization on his own family agency. Before this he found there had been a kind of unconscious barrier set up —"a psychological block"—with regard to older persons. They had been relegated to the bottom of the heap. Facing the fact that workers found it more interesting to work with marital problems than with the problems of the elderly, he saw the attitudes of caseworkers as yet little different from the attitudes of the lay community.

And again, three years later, he was saying the same thing about caseworker attitudes and feelings, imploring the profession to examine its own feelings about older people and about aging in general.

---

*A point noted more recently by economists such as Juanita Kreps, but rarely by social workers.

I venture to say that most of us feel that older persons are stubborn, set in their ways, and so psychologically oriented that they are incapable of movement and change. Our feelings may be shaped by our own fear of aging—fear for ourselves and our contemporaries. It is a state of being most caseworkers have not yet experienced and hence cannot identify with. In many instances, experiences we may have had with our parents and relatives were negative and conflict producing. Our struggle for separation in earlier years often prevents us—in our new-found personal strength—from thinking about those we have separated from.

As caseworkers we are as subject to these attitudes as are all others. This may explain in part why casework in the field of the aged is less developed than in any other field of social work . . . Caseworkers, too, have veered away from pioneering effort in this field. The reasons for this can be found among those attitudes and feelings mentioned above in addition to others peculiar to caseworkers by virtue of their experience and practice. Among these must be mentioned the view held by many caseworkers that work with the aged cannot be very rewarding. We are dealing here with persons who are in the "ending phase" of life; with those who are about to die and who, therefore, supposedly do not wish change.[6]

Although Posner found in reviewing the developments of the 1940–1950 decade that the greatest advance had taken place in the attitudes of casework agencies and caseworkers themselves, he still felt it was only a beginning, that caseworkers really held little belief in the creative potentialities of the older person:

The truth is—if we are ready to admit it to ourselves —that most family caseworkers have not seen the challenge in work with the aged that they have seen in work with children and young families.

We speak of family casework as involving the whole family including, presumably, the older person; we speak of generics in casework which, if I am correct, implies equal concern for the old as well as the young, and yet we must admit that our interest and our fascination has been for the young and not for the old. We think of the young in terms of growth and change, but when it comes to the older person our thought and feeling processes veer in the direction of deterioration and death. It is almost as if in spite of our undifferentiated view of family casework, we have separated out the older person not in terms of understanding him better or to view him as one requiring special concern and skill in handling, but rather as one who somehow does not fit into our accustomed pattern of practice.

Perhaps it would be too harsh to say that, professionally speaking, we have relegated the older person to the scrapheap. But in practical terms that is what we have done. Let us look at our caseloads to see. . . . At best the attitude of family agencies and workers has been one of tolerance rather than one of acceptance. It is almost as if caseworkers have operated on the basis of a "get rid of" philosophy rather than a "take on" philosophy.[7]

There is a growing sense of impatience on this subject of caseworkers, social workers, convictions, and he becomes less gentle:

Our institutions for the aged specialize in working with older people. Yet in this day and age [1955] one might as well look for a needle in a haystack as for a caseworker in the majority of homes for the aged. We have done much to improve our plants and our medical and nursing care but one would think that older people had no feelings, no psychological needs, no reactions they need help with.* We make the assumption that older people will-

---

*This, of course, is an area that has seen much growth since 1955, in both quantity and quality. As the Director of Social Services for The De Paul Retirement Apartment & Mount St. Vincent Nursing Center run by the Sisters of Providence in Seattle, I can personally attest the existence of institutions well aware of the feelings and psychological needs of the aged and infirm, focused on making last years good years.

ingly enter a home for the aged to enjoy the country
club atmosphere and that all problems cease once admission has been gained—remembering, of course, that only
a selected few have the privilege of entering.[8]

He goes on, showing how we do not serve older people
and asking why. And asking again and again that we look
behind our complacence, especially where some accomplishments have been made. He will not let us deny that most of
us have unresolved conflicts in this area, that "we have been
young but not old," and are uneasy with our own unknowns.
But he emphasizes for the caseworker who works in this
field, an opportunity is offered to struggle with his attitudes
towards aging and to achieve a balance which gives him
a real sense of his own problem as well as an opportunity
for change.

In a way that makes one feel the questions began with
himself, Posner asks questions—probing questions. He gets
to some of them in the agency manual but first there was a
statement of understanding that caseworkers belonged to
a new, young, vigorous profession, that they were mostly
preoccupied with finding new ways of helping, with learning new skills, with a continuous process of exploration
and testing. Because of this they feared that work with
elderly people would deprive them of the stimulus gener-
ated by the fast tempo and momentum. The preconceived
notion that older people change more slowly, and that the
ratio of effective casework with elderly people is minimal,
tended to keep workers away from this field. With positive
portrayals of older people receiving less attention than
negative ones, caseworkers feared to apply their helping
skills to older persons. In another of the almost "side-
thoughts" dropped by Posner, rarely mentioned elsewhere,
and yet the seed of something yet to come, he saw in the
caseworkers' fear of meeting the frustrations of working
with the old a forgetting and overlooking that younger
people, too, put up tremendous barriers against being
helped.

Then the questions for the uneasy answers:

The most outstanding and most frightful impact that
the thought of "old age" has upon us is the fact that in
working with older people we necessarily must think of
the ending phase of life—of death. How many of us can
truly accept death as part of life? How many of us can
generally accept any finality? Yet is there any greater
reality than the finality of death? While living, we are not
moved by death but by life. Does it not follow, then, if
as caseworkers, devoted to the task of helping people to
"live" as long as they are "alive," that it is our responsibility to help people to live to the very last? Many of us
are prompted to concentrate on helping elderly people
because we feel almost "sorry" for them; we feel that
they are frequently so totally rejected by their environment that we want to make up, so to say, for the "evils"
of the world. Yet as disciplined professional people we
know that "pity" does not help people to mobilize themselves. Therefore, if we attempt to answer only our own
personal need to find an answer for our "attitude of
pity," we hamper all possibilities of help.[9]

As he asked his own agency staff, and as he had already
asked himself, he went on later to ask such questions in
one of his last speeches to fellow helping professionals.
Discussing what he felt were the main issues involved with
casework with the aging in 1960, he said that what seemed
most important was a critical evaluation of casework problems and practices to look for the difficulties that kept
agencies from letting go of traditional ways of working in
order to give more sensitive help to aging clients and their
families. He asked for a good clear look into individual
helping hearts, into agency policies, into schools of training, to find out why they were blocked from developing
new practices and services for new client needs.

By now it had been twelve years since he had begun to
talk about attitudes. He had persistently hammered the
thought wherever he could that it was not only "they" the

society, but "we" the helpers who needed to stop and notice
where we were before we could go on. Here he has a more
professional approach, hitting at something dear to professionals—their use of the subjective as they face any issue.
Longing for them to see that our subjective feelings matter
with the old, too:

> The first question I should like to present has to do
> with attitudes. This is a constant favorite with me and
> I have discussed this at other times in a variety of con-
> texts. I am less concerned at the moment with the atti-
> tudes of society as a whole toward aging or older persons.
> These have been treated quite adequately in the litera-
> ture, although to the extent that social work and social
> workers are creatures of our society the whole subject
> is of great importance.

> Now in casework we lay great stress upon the case-
> worker's subjective attitudes. Indeed it is understood quite
> clearly that they must be reckoned with in dealing with
> clients of all age groups and all types of problems, and
> that unless they are properly understood they may well
> impede the application of casework principles to all
> clients.

> Equally important are the attitudes of agencies. Agen-
> cies, as you know, are anything but inanimate and I have
> no problem in suggesting that in helping clients the sub-
> jective attitudes of the social agency—including its poli-
> cies and procedures, its traditions of service, the way it
> provides the service, its auspices, its view about the
> standards of service—are basically important in deter-
> mining the help we give.

> Today we take this fundamental view for granted. This
> was not always so. In the history of social work and
> social institutions subjective attitudes of workers and
> agencies were not always related to the better under-
> standing of the client or in offering better service. In a
> society which made a virtue of protecting the poor, the
> weak, the sick, and the friendless, subjective attitudes of

workers—often negative in nature—were disguised as love and respect.

And is he not asking—are we, too, putting on but a mask of love and respect?

Perhaps in retrospect we look upon these "protective" attitudes and the institutions developed to care for those who need our help as cruel and unhuman. In social work, in particular, as we have learned to recognize the meaning of help and the differential values of certain settings we have often gone beyond the pace of society itself to develop different forms and methods of care. The child care field is probably one of the best examples of this type of attitudinal change.

As we look upon casework with the aging, however, we find, surprisingly enough, that we have not given as much thought to our subjective attitudes as we have in other areas of work. How else can we explain the fact that few aged persons, percentage-wise, receive service in our family agencies than do other age groups? How else explain the fact that in spite of the demonstrated need for special types of services for the aged and their families, few such services have been developed in family agencies?

Far be it from me to question the family agency's concerns about the aging. The concerns are there as well as a real awareness of the new social problems that have arisen in the past decades. But has it kept pace by way of developing new knowledge, skills, and techniques in helping older people and their families?

. . . The family agency's "belief in people" has historically never been based upon a policy of exclusiveness, but rather upon one which has recognized the needs of all people regardless of age or condition. Yet, any careful observer of the family agency scene would have to admit that they are far from being all encompassing—at least as far as the aged client is concerned. . . . Whether it is the caseworker or the agency, I think it is quite clear

by now that the attitudinal component is one of the
barriers to giving effective service to older persons and
their families. It appears that no matter how much
research has been done to demonstrate otherwise, we
still hold little belief in the creative potentialities of the
older person and that most of us do not see the same
challenge in work with the aged that we see in work
with children. . . . We have not yet come to grips by
relating our theories of growth and change to those we
feel are in the ending phase of life. . . . Is age in itself a
factor which makes for this kind of technical aversion?
Is it our fear of aging? Is it related to our own parental
problems? Is it the internalization of the old stereotype
of the older person's need for protection and isolation
which prevents us from seeing him as one who has the
same common human needs as others? Is it our own fear
of death—an element which inevitably plays a role in
the way we use ourselves with clients? Is it a fear of our
own future—illness, insecurity, loss of loved ones, loneliness that seems to take hold of us and prevents us from
using our dynamic processes with older clients?[10]

And so he asks the questions of different audiences, of
different readers, in different years, with ever more urgency.
In this same address he goes on to dwell more on the one
aspect of loneliness that comes between us and our service
through our attitude, and quotes from Dr. Frieda Fromm-
Reichmann's essay on "Loneliness"[11] in which she states the
psychiatrist's dilemma, one that he applies to social workers
as well, of finding loneliness such a painful, frightening
experience that practically everything is done to avoid it.
This evading includes that of workers and writers who
might otherwise be clarifying and using and truly helping
the state they evade. What he found most meaningful was
that a painful subject like loneliness—or any painful aspect
of life—was not merely something we try to avoid, which
may be very natural, but the professional people who most
need to thoughtfully face the painful also have a tendency
to avoid thinking about it or studying it or using it in practice. This was the crux of what he tried to convey.

It is the crux of what he had been trying to convey all along, a part of the psychological block accepted as fact from his first article on, but fought throughout. In essence, his main question was not expressed as such. Instead it was there in a simple statement of the fact that it is difficult for young caseworkers to recognize and accept that old age is just as important a time of life as any other period of life.

Old age is just as important a time of life as any other period of life. Therein is the ringing question—do we really believe, deep in each helping heart, do we really believe?

Notes

1. William Posner, "Casework with the Aged as a Specialized Service in a Multiple Service Agency," Jewish Community Services of Long Island (1952), p. 2.

2. ———, "Older Years, Enriching Years," *Journal of the Long Island Consultation Center* (January 1960), p. 6.

3. ———, "Meeting the Needs of the Aged in the Community," Council of Jewish Federations and Welfare Funds (Atlantic City, March 1953), p. 1.

4. Abraham Myerson, "The Conflict between the Old and the New Generations," *The Family* III (November 1922), p. 5.

5. William Posner and Rochelle Indelman, "Jewish Community Services of Long Island—Manual of Policies and Procedures in the Division of Services for the Aged," March 1956, pp. 4–5.

6. William Posner, "Casework Process in a Private Residence Program for Older Persons," *Journal of Social Work Process* 4 (May 1953), pp. 9–28.

7. ———, "Casework with the Aged as a Specialized Service in a Multiple Service Agency," op. cit., p. 5.

8. ———, "New Horizons in Casework with the Aged," Institute on New Horizons for Casework with the Aged (New York, March 1955), p. 5.

9. William Posner and Rochelle Indelman, op. cit., p. 5.

10. William Posner, "Characteristics of Casework with Older People—A Discussion of Basic Issues," Seminar of the National Committee on the Aging, Harriman, New York, October 1960, p. 18.

11. Frieda Fromm-Reichmann, "Loneliness," *Psychiatry* (February 1959).

..... about understanding and response

IT WAS SAID OF Posner that he was a man of "all heart," but the rich quality of caring and compassion that runs through his words and his life is neither cloying nor sentimental. Always along with it is the inquiring mind, the seeking to learn, the reach for understanding. What is it like to be old, he wanted to know and then to tell. In his outline of need for the new—in attitude, understanding, acceptance, action—the implication is that we must first amend our attitudes and review our values in order to understand. And yet, what he found and relayed out of his own need to know had an effect on the attitudes of those whose lives he touched. The action taken in agency and field influenced attitude and revised understanding. Posner realized that the path from attitude to action might indeed be from action to attitude and back, a spiralling circle beginning wherever we are.

Although this section is meant to dwell upon an understanding of older people, values refuse to be left behind and action must be involved in his descriptions of desirable response to understanding in ways of handling what we learn. We look, we learn, we understand. And if that understanding is accepted as true, we respond and our response is an action. Without it understanding would mean nothing.

A large portion of Posner's work dealt with understanding the particular characteristics of the elderly, the unique qualities and reactions that distinguish them from other ages, but he found as a first necessary step toward such understanding a recognition that there *are* differences. Granting the danger of overlooking the common, there were still for him two important ways to aid in the discernment of the differences—by specialization in working with particular types only, and by special emphasis on individuals within the general type.

Specialization

Posner came to the Jewish Community Services of Long Island as supervisor of their Services for the Aged soon after such services had been established as a separate, specialized unit of service. It was unusual at that time and has yet to become common, although there is presently increasing interest on the social work education side in what is now called concentration of focus. He soon became convinced of its merit and proclaimed the value of such concentration at various times to various audiences.

Immediately we see the intertwining of understanding and attitude and action. Here specialization, an action, is also a way toward understanding, and understanding a way toward a change of attitude. The practice aspect will be dealt with later, but for now it must be at least mentioned as it was so much a part of his thinking on gaining insight.

After just a few years of experience, recognizing that most family agencies operate on a unifying philosophy feeling that any type of separation of the family within the agency leads only to an artificial separation and segmentation which has little validity in actual practice, he emphasized that due to the attitude of the workers, specialization was essential. Without it, the old aged case would continue the case receiving the last and least attention. But it was not just one way to deal with the situation as it was, it was also a way toward growth. The likeness of older persons to other human beings was agreed upon. It was then necessary to work at recognizing the differences, learning more about them, reaching new specialized knowledge, techniques and skills for serving the increasing numbers of aged coming for help.

Throughout the years that followed, Posner, wherever he had someone to heed, reported on the progress of the program and its growing benefits in changing understanding and feelings on the part of the caseworkers involved. Based on the conviction that fundamental social work principles were not sufficient to evaluate the life situations of older persons or to comprehend the personality dynamics motivating them in their quests for help, the new specialized department had been instituted. What they hoped for, happened. By sheer concentration new thinking, new skills and values, new programs were developed.

Individualization

Posner was a man of charity and a hard-working man. A social worker, all that he wrote drew on his convictions about basic social work principles. The one that most shines out and is so pervasive as to require special mention was individualization founded on the dignity and difference of each individual. It was a part of his plea against stereotyping. He started with it, he returned to it again and again, and he ended with it.

The process of getting older is as universal as any basic factor governing the life of a human being. It is a process which involves all persons, no matter under which circumstances or conditions they live. The whole concept of time seen from the point of view of a life-span is involved here. Getting older is as unavoidable as breathing is unavoidable for living. A distinction, however, must be made between getting older and "aging." The process of "aging" is not a universal one. This phase of life varies from human being to human being in all its aspects. Commonly speaking, "aging" connotes gradual mental and physical disintegration. While each and every one of us, by virtue of living, is getting older, not each and every one of us is "aging." We bring this concept to the foreground because we feel this to be the core of our ability to individualize elderly people and to help them accordingly.[1]

In these and other words of staff instruction, there was a recognition of our responsibility to see each person asking for help—regardless of age—as a living person with rights and capacities and with hopes and fears. There was an air of excitement about the possibilities and potentials of the individual person that he expressed whenever he spoke or wrote. Working with the aging could be a challenge in just this breaking through the category into the individual soul. The problems might be similar—loss of status, job, home, health. The ambivalence might always be there between a desire for independence and a reality of increasing dependence. Most older people might be facing a gradually narrowing world with apprehension over diminishing strengths. But common though the needs may be, and similar the circumstances, the individual is unique. The excitement of challenge is offered in the search for the particular strengths and potential of each. The older person with the problem is what he is as a result of both his past history and present reality, as a result of inner and outer stresses. Has the problem developed from the inner personality pattern or from a reaction to outer attitudes and pressures? It is for those who seek to help to seek first to know and understand.

When he did his major study of past literature in 1958, he brought out the same kind of emphasis by others. He quoted from Grace Browning who had said that the aged are not a type any more than the unemployed are a type, that they stand out as personalities, "each the product of his own life experiences and the prey of his individual hopes, fears, and necessitous circumstances."[2] And in reviewing the question of the symbolic meaning of the requests made by older clients, Posner saw many older people tending to deny advancing age or the loss of functions that they are unable to face. We can recognize the desire to be coddled and to receive sympathy. But if we understand the emotional needs that underlie any person's behavior this pattern can some-

times be modified. It is our tendency to classify or stereotype these patterns that makes for difficulty.

Typically, Posner does not stop at stating the need or
pointing out the difficulty, but digs deeper, and again ties
the difficulty in individualizing the aged to the difficulty
with our attitude.

> For not to do this [change our subjective attitudes]
> may very well obscure the fact that the aged person does
> require an individualized consideration of his needs, and
> understanding of his individual strengths and weaknesses
> as well as those factors that are real for the group as a
> whole. It may obscure for the worker the fact that older
> persons' needs too are varied and changing. A hopeless
> and static approach to aging may diminish our aware-
> ness that motivations, aspirations, the need for self-
> esteem, and the existence of defenses against their impair-
> ment, influence the behavior of the older client in family
> relationships, in reaction to changes in living arrange-
> ments, to hospitalization, to institutionalization, to the
> requests he brings to social agencies.[3]

So, with the structure of specialization and the leaven of
individualization, what are these factors that are real for
the group of aging as a whole? In various articles and
through his progressing times, Posner set forth different sets
of those specific characteristics found in working with older
people. In the beginning—and the first article that put them
in outlined form was in 1952—those listed were mainly the
more obvious ones; later with his experience, sensitivity,
and expanding awareness, there were more that involved
not just the facts of aging, but the internal and emotional
meanings. "What is it really like to be old?" he continued
to ask. And to answer.

CHARACTERISTICS

1. *Age Itself.*

Always the first factor is simply that the person is of
older years and knows it and feels it. We have seen that old

age has a distinct cultural and psychological meaning in
our society. People view old age with fear and dread. As
for the older person himself, he has in many instances in-
ternalized the general rejection of age as a rejection of
himself and has become emotionally insecure in his own
living.

Posner saw the age factor as a challenge and a focus. It
became for him the very implement we concentrate on and
use in working with the aged. Through understanding the
client's particular psychology and seeing his individual
reaction to age, we can utilize our casework skills to help
him.

The internalizing of external attitudes was to Posner the
real difference in age itself as a factor of human personality.
He saw their emotional problems not as inherent but related
to the frustrations and insecurities created by those attitudes
previously mentioned that label the old useless and un-
wanted. As a result, it is difficult for us to discern the balance in the individual between inner and outer stresses,
when the outer have become inner.

2. *Death.*

Death is a fact of life for everyone but its inevitable
imminence is a fact with a difference for older people. Dealing with those who are about to die means facing death as
a daily fact with all the feelings that facing death has for
the client and for ourselves. Is there fear or confidence,
dread or hope? What is each individual finding in this closing
of the life process and how is he using this part of life
called death? Here we are involved with the older person's
gradually narrowing world, his apprehension over diminishing strengths and the finality of a death that comes daily
closer.

Posner asked workers to look squarely at what it might
mean to an individual to be dying, questions that had been
previously ignored or left to the church men. It was easier
to soothe, to comfort, to help deny the inevitable. Today

with the recent writings of Dr. Elisabeth Kubler-Ross and others we are becoming aware that the answers to such questions *can* lead to more helpful ways, and that the beginning of help is in facing our own feelings first, a route that Posner consistently recommended.

3. *Intensification.*

Often the older person becomes preoccupied with death, or with religions that emphasize judgment or immortality, or with himself and the fundamental aspects of his physical being such as eating and eliminating and breathing and heart-beating that signal a continuation of life. Posner used "intensification" to describe the prevalent characteristic of the aged manifested in the narrow absorption, the near obsession on particular subjects. As usual he sought to understand what was behind the tendency it describes and what to do about it. He did not find it proven by experience that older persons are more interested in religion than younger people are. He found instead an intensification of previous attitudes and practices. With money and possessions, as with religion, things that had always mattered to some degree became even more important in the new circumstances of age and insecurity. To the degree that such attitudes and feelings enable the client to live securely, he felt they were to be encouraged.

One of the important lessons learned in working with older people was that all of these factors—which may hold for all persons—manifested themselves in an exaggerated form. Attitudes towards money for example—the need of an older person who no longer feels accepted in the labor market to have a reserve—come through more sharply than in casework with younger persons. Death and funeral arrangements, too, become a valid concern. And reminiscence, the "classic" content of an older person's conversation, displays the need to tell of an importance and influence in younger years. Such near obsessions must be accepted as right and necessary for the older person.

The intensification of interest in oneself known as narcissism is often taken for granted in analyzing older people. Posner denied the assumption. On the contrary, he saw the normal aging person as having a capacity for a giving kind of love and an abundance of personality characteristics expressing themselves altruistically toward those younger and older. The trouble comes when the offering is not accepted— by the younger generation especially. Even such a small thing as a smile unnoticed or received without response may close a door that had been open.

In other words, narcissism can develop as a defense against rejection, but it need not follow that the seeds of generosity and outgoing interest are not still alive for growth given the opportunity.

4. *Illness.*

The opportunity for giving is often limited by diminishing resources and by the state of health. Working with older clients usually means working with ill people. It is the rule rather than the exception. Posner found this a decided difference from the majority of family agency clients. Dealing with it requires a particular kind of understanding of the kinds and stages of physical illness and the specific effects of the ailments on the emotions as well as the physical and mental functioning of an individual.

It requires, too, an understanding of the emotional effect of illness on spirit and energy, and he begins to look for better ways of using the illness itself as a tool toward growth. We are reminded that physical illness may be common among the old due to degenerative processes, but we must not assume that at the same time there is a similar change in the older person's emotional stability or his ability to feel pleasure and pain, warmth and security.

The subjects of self-determination and decision-making follow later, but here as they relate to illness, he found that frequently people who have become dependent as a result of illness are very resigned and ready to accept anything. Since such resignation is not conducive to physical improvement, if we go along with it we actually do not accomplish much. Instead we must deliberately use our understanding with the client to motivate renewed active involvement in his own continuing life and the lives of others.

There's another danger, too, in looking at illness. Five years after stating he found illness the rule rather than the exception, experience and study of unfolding research seem to have altered Posner's view somewhat:

> We often think of older persons as sick people. Percentage-wise it may be true that old people suffer more from chronic illness than persons of other age groups. Yet, if we apply our generic social work principles, we would undoubtedly see illness in the older person as a very relative matter. Social workers with experience in the field know how frequently illness is used as a basis for the older person's defensive behavior. Illness, after all, is becoming to an older person; it is part of the cultural stereotype. One of the real challenges in work with older people, therefore, is working with illness and helping to differentiate that which is real and that which is symptomatic of defensive mechanisms.[4]

5. *Tempo.*

Although not all degenerative processes involve illness, with most people they do mean a slowing down of tempo physically and mentally. It means the older client may need more time to react emotionally and to heal physically. It may mean patience on the part of the caseworker. It may mean a change of procedure by the agency. It may mean to the old person himself a feeling of being left behind while youth and our changing society rush on by.

It also means a slow movement toward small goals, because along with the decreased pace of mental reactions is what some see as just a stubborn resistance to change. Posner saw it instead as a natural reluctance toward the new stemming from firmly established patterns developed through the many years of living. One of the greatest obstacles to overcome is to think less of goals in helping older persons, goals that more often than not may be unattainable, and more in terms of helping the older person to use himself more effectively within his limited situation.

In advance of his time, Posner saw the increasing value given to short-time help where dramatic changes sometimes resulted, but also saw the danger of its application to the aged because such drama rarely occurs with older persons. Instead there must be an aim toward one little thing at a time in all the steps of talking and relating and acting that are involved in the helping ways. Then small changes in themselves can appear as dramatic in light of the life-long patterns and attitudes that older people must give up to accept any change at all.

One of these life-long patterns, at least in our present times, is a reticence about speaking of personal matters to strangers. It is rarely easy to draw an older person into revealing the deep feelings and conflicts and hurts and sorrows. Nor is it easy, having found a problem, to stay with small goals when we tend to compare this work with work with children who have a life ahead and who may make our investment more noticeably worth something. And yet, in our comparing, we must remember the fact that casework has never thought in terms of unlimited goals, but rather in terms of helping the individual in line with his limited capacities and capabilities.

Posner puts "partialization" as a necessary outgrowth of the slowed tempo of thought and movement toward change:

> Our understanding of casework process generally and our knowledge of helping people has given us ample evidence to believe that most people find it difficult to take help or to make adjustments in a total and all-encompassing way. Stating this in its simplest form, we do not expect a client to be able to develop a relationship with his worker or to be able to recognize his feelings in coming to an agency for help in, let us say, one interview. To

expect this would be to expect the client to master the totality of this new and often fearful situation. To help a client to relate to his request for service, and to recognize his feelings, it is necessary to break up the totality as it were or to "partialize" the elements that go into the request for help. . . . We cannot prevent clients from total reactions, but we can—at least through the process of partialization—help them to react less totally to the service given them.[5]

What he emphasizes is the link between the fact that having lived a long life full of many changes often means a reluctance about more change and the fact that whatever change is necessitated or hoped for necessarily requires a tempo on our part to match the slower tempo on theirs.

Psychologically, as we have seen previously, the older person has more difficulty in engaging himself in a process which involves the possibility of change. We may add that any older person who is, so to say, in the ending phase of life, has a right to be more fearful of change. The older person *needs* to know that he has a little more time at his disposal to examine and to work on his problem toward a different solution. But the older person, like a younger one, welcomes some definition and framework within which to function. Time often becomes the most realistic and dynamic element which brings the "older client" together with the agency worker.[6]

Again you see the route of this man's thinking. Understanding never ends at passive understanding. It becomes the active tool to use in helping.

6. *Separation.*

Working with the older client brings us face to face with problems of separation. To no other client or group of clients coming to the family agency does this problem apply so generally. For family agencies especially, most older clients or adult children seeking help are considering some form of

separation. Because of this Posner saw a need to carefully
discern with increasing understanding those situations where
the request for separation was real, as opposed to those
where it was symptomatic of other problems, where it was
really a request for another type of help. Again he called for
clarification of the worker's own attitude, this time toward
separations. Only in facing and working through our own
similar problems can we help clients with theirs.

Here he was talking about the immediate problem of
many an older client—a new separation, recent or imminent.
But throughout he spoke of our need to understand the
effects of all the separations, all the accumulated losses a
person faces as he moves along in life. By the time of later
life, the number has probably increased . . . loss of youth
certainly, loss of health to some degree, loss of beauty, of
work, of strength, of mate, of family, of friends, of home,
and soon the loss of life itself. What *are* the emotional reactions and how can we help and how can we learn to help
more?

Sometimes the emptiness of later years is caused more by
loss of role than by the other losses. It is not only the result
of retirement or the new physical limitations that prevent
one from doing what one did before. It is a part of the
internalizing of the external attitude that there is really no
reason for being when one no longer has the same part to
play in family or business or community. The importance
of role in all social work and psychological studies and
treatments is taken for granted now. The concept was in its
beginning stages when Posner was seeing the older client
as one who was seeking a role to play in society and who
needed help in finding the proper role for himself.

His view of the need for more study on providing specific
and practical roles will be brought in later, but in the meantime, so much of what he writes is concerned with simply
acknowledging and respecting the older person as a person
of worth, one who is not apart from society but still a part
of it. By working with the problems and limitations present,

by alleviating those we can alleviate for people who have for so long been denied a sense of worth, it may be the beginning of a new sense of self.

Giving a feeling of worth was one way to counteract the pain of losses. Perhaps every helpful method mentioned is meant in some way to make up for losses, to help people live with the losses they've had and to face those that come. Another way Posner saw as effective in dealing with the suffering of separation was to provide continuity. He mentioned it frequently, usually side by side with outreach.

Continuity in working with the older client meant especially sustaining a continuing casework contact wherever possible from beginning to end. Motivation is low at best with many a person seeking help. The fear of seeking help in light of other rejections isn't easy to overcome. There is sometimes the practical stumbling block of being unable to get to an agency. To these add the reticence to speak in any personal way with strangers, the slow building of relationship, and the one stability of a continuing and caring caseworker in an unstable world acquires a special importance. This will also mean leaving the usual professional pattern and going out to reach for the client to better make real for him our warmth and acceptance, our desire to accord him special worth.

7. *Loneliness and Depression.*

Perhaps from a strange land, or a stranger in the current culture of his own country, perhaps with an abyss of misunderstanding in his family, often with painful losses, the older person is often more vulnerable than most to the problems of loneliness and depression. Certainly they are problems too common with older people to be set aside with simple sympathy. As obvious above, Posner was concerned at our hesitation to explore such troublesome areas. But they do exist, and we must go on into the places that hurt in order to heal.

Where loneliness is concerned, we help in many of the

ways already mentioned—in the relationship, the continuity, the understanding, the individualizing, the enhancement of the sense of self. But there is much yet to be done in increasing our perception of ways of communication. It is not uncommon to hear of treating older people like children, talking to them as one talks to a child. This is not Posner's answer to bridging the gap of communication between generations, and although much had been accomplished, he looked forward to better ways of communication, better ways of entering into loneliness.

For depression, for lifting the bruised spirits, Posner saw first the need for recognizing its base in loss, and then for using the material available within the clients themselves, their own strengths and spiritual resources. Our part is mainly to assist them to understand themselves and to face their own abilities and limitations realistically. In favoring a clear look at alternatives (providing the social scene is advanced enough to allow alternatives), he wanted the client to put feelings aside long enough to see the situation clearly. Facts can so often dispel fears.

8. *Dependence.*

Posner was aware of the ambivalence of the elderly person about independence and dependence. It is there where family relations are concerned, where money is a question, sometimes in housing problems, often with failing health, almost always in seeking help. His account of a particular person involved with a decision about going into a foster home, describes specifically the dependence factor for general application:

> The struggle this client is going through appears clear enough. One does not easily give up independence and the fear of the unknown is greater still. Mrs. Fels is worried about her visual impairment and fears it might become worse and that she will then be unable to live alone. Should she give up now or continue alone as long as possible? She also has a financial problem. Is that the

focus and is it basically a fear of getting financial help or does she really want placement? The agency's clarity about the help it can give, and what it cannot, helps the client to focus on what she considers to be the basic service she wants. There is a continuous testing out and almost a wish to have a decision made for her. But this will not do—neither for the client nor the agency. No one can really take the struggle out of Mrs. Fels' hands. She will have to decide; no one can really do it for her. The agency, however, can accept her indecision and is ready to have the client return. The recognition of the client's strength remains a basic principle in work with an older person.[7]

Here are two areas of response to an understanding of the client's feelings. First, using our understanding in being aware of the client's reactions to seeking or receiving help; and secondly, a determined insistence on self-determination. He was, of course, especially interested in the reactions involved in requesting placement in the private residence program he was so instrumental in developing. He was even more specifically concerned with the older person's part in the decision making. His statements about planning placements when the move is to a private home are equally applicable for any move—to a nursing home or other institution, to a small apartment from one's own house, to a retirement home or community.

Placement away from one's own home or one's established way of living requires a degree of separation at once traumatic and fearful to the older client and his family. Although the older person may have experienced various types of separation in his life, his coming to an agency for placement has in it implications of a "last mile" psychology. . . . There is a recognition in this coming that he has reached a stage of dependence which he did not have before. The degree of this feeling, or sometimes the lack of it, will vary with the client's immediate experience prior to his request for help. Many older persons have for years lived with adult children. These persons surprisingly enough look upon placement as a move toward the reestablishment of long lost independence and security. For in living with their children they had experienced a striking reversal of roles. It was their children who took care of them, who supplied them with daily necessities, who supplied them with money and clothing and food. They had lost their traditional parental role to their children. The inability any longer to live with their children is in most instances a result of this struggle for reassertion of role and for independence. . . . To the older person who does not live with his children but who has maintained his own living independence, application for placement will more nearly emphasize feelings of dependence and futility. Usually, the request for placement is made at the point where the client begins to feel physically unable to take care of all his personal needs. . . . To this person, coming to the agency for help in placement will precipitate considerable struggle in an effort to hold on to as much independence as possible. The ambivalent feelings of not wanting to give up what he has, and yet having to face the reality of a change, will usually bring forth an expression of distrust, centered on procedures or on the whole placement function.[8]

The above applies, of course, not only to the old clients' feelings about contacting an agency about placement, but to any first contact they make for a helping hand. In Posner's experience with specialization they had always wondered why, in the face of the increasing number of older persons in the population, so few were availing themselves of agency help. After the establishment of their special service, they realized many older people could not be expected to come for service entirely on their own as did younger people. Older people did not come for help because they feared the same rejections they had experienced in employment, in housing, and in other areas of living. They did not come— not because they did not need help, but because they felt they would be misunderstood as they were by their children and by the community at large, because they feared yet another loss of control.

So most older people come for help fearfully, fearful of their reception, fearful of taking a step that may mean a change in the status of their independence. To reassure them promptly—not only of our respect for them as individuals—but of their right to self-determination, their right to keep that portion of independence that allows making one's own choice, Posner's staff was instructed to make clear immediately just who the client was, and where the responsibility for decision lay. He had no use for being overly protective and saw it in families as their own defense against the guilt they found in their feelings. In describing the first interview with an older client whose daughter had already been denied her desire to handle her mother's situation directly with the agency:

> This first interview, although exploratory in nature, reveals some of the basic concepts that assume importance in working with older persons. One such element is to emphasize again in concrete terms that the older person is our primary client. Seeing Mrs. Benson, the mother, alone and first gave emphasis to this fact. Although she is hardly an inhibited person, being able to talk with the worker alone gave her a sense of freedom she could not otherwise have. She can air her complaints about her children and come to a decision herself about the service she requests.[9]

As is so often true in social work, the categories chosen here as a frame for setting forth the opinions and principles of Posner are not always clear and distinct with black and white lines between. Rather the boundaries are vague and the points of one portion frequently overlap into another. Such is the case in discussing the older person's right of choice and the older person's relationship with children, to follow. As a link between the two:

> We want to give the older person a sense of security and responsibility for himself. We want to develop a

sense of independence in both young and old, so that
their own lives become emotionally stable and secure
without the need for imposing their will on each other.
It is only through the security of each that satisfactory
inter-relationships can be developed.[10]

9. *The Generational Component.*

This was an area where Posner's thought began with the
dependence of an older adult on his adult children. What
does it mean to be led and protected by the children you
once bred and guided? The change of roles was but one
facet of many that developed into what Posner termed the
generational component. Each person is a part of a generation, and being in that generation is a part of each person.
How does it affect him in his relations at any one time with
persons of the same or a different generation? Since the
time of his writing, such thoughts have unfolded into one
of the major psychological issues of the late '60s and
early '70s.

In his first article, centered on a description of the private
residence program, he makes it clear that adult children are
not permitted to make decisions for their parents unless necessitated by undeniable mental incapacity, but that the involvement of adult children in the planning is essential.
Acknowledging the need for the two generations to continue to work together as parts of a whole family, he insisted
that the person with the problem was the primary client,
and the problem was most often that of the old person
himself.

It doesn't take many words to describe this policy, but
the ramifications are many and they touch a variety of
hidden, perhaps repressed emotions. In the case description
and discussion involving the placement of a woman who
had been living with her adult daughter, it was found that
the agency requirements brought out not only the expected
guilt feelings of the daughter, but the underlying hostility
of both. The task may be centered on the older person, but
the worker by no means uses a one-sided approach. The

older person is frequently dependent in some aspect of his life, financially or otherwise, upon other members of his family. Although the older person continues to be the primary client, the agency's concern must go beyond the one to include the important others in the life of the one. These children, relatives, responsible friends Posner termed secondary clients. For their sakes as well as for the sake of the older client, he felt they had to be given the opportunity to understand agency aims, what to expect and what might be expected of them in the care and support of the central client.

He recognized and respected the limits of the adult child's ability to assume responsibility and the very real damage that can be done to both if the emotional motivations are founded on old and now unreal ties. Openness was strongly encouraged. In requesting help to find another living arrangement for the parent, there is so often a sore place full of guilt within the adult child. Out of it comes the desire to have just anyone else tell the parent a separation is necessary, but Posner knew that facing the parent directly with the fact was something the adult child had to do. If he didn't, there could develop only two sore places. If he did, hopefully with the help of the agency, the one could be healed.

Later . . . . in this interview we see a continuation of Mrs. Glick's [Mrs. Benson's adult daughter] real change both in herself and with respect to the other relationships in placement. She recognizes her previous feelings as representative of her need to rebel, to fight. She had to do this because she lacked a sense of self, a sense of her own worth as a person. She was insecure in relation to her mother, to the agency, and to the residence owner, and thought she could gain security by fighting everybody. The caseworker helped her to recognize that all of this represented her own insecurity, her own inability to feel.

In venting her hostility and her mixed feelings and in getting assurance from the worker, Mrs. Glick is able to accept her role—herself—so much better. She is able to feel, and there is a tenderness about her. Doing for her mother is now less complicated by feelings of guilt. These feelings have been replaced by a sense of responsibility. There is room for compromise, for reaching out to her mother. . . . In her new-found security she can actually feel happy in doing for her mother and for herself.[11]

The search is for a clarification of the right and reasonable responsibilities, the achievement of a friendly emancipation at this point just as a reverse emancipation was a part of family development a generation before. Only then can the adult child define his proper role—as an adult child rather than as a super-parent. Looking with the worker at the parent as a responsible person and the central client hopefully will develop a new perspective and attitude for the adult child.

As can be seen from the above, implicit in the service to the aged is service to the entire family. Satisfactory or not, the older person's relationship with adult children is there and not to be set aside. Working always toward a strengthening of families and a prevention of family breakdown was not just for young or middle-aged adults with young or adolescent children. It was for help to older adults geared simultaneously to the adult children as well. Yet Posner had no intention of taking from adult children their responsibilities toward their parents. Rather he wanted to clarify and facilitate the ways of being responsible without psychological damage to the varied generations involved.

It is grounded in Posner's belief in the individual, this emphasis on the need to probe the parental relationships. The policies and practices described in early articles show encouragement of affectionate separateness between generations—generations that may well be willingly tied but need not be unwillingly bound. In later articles, he continued to explore the meanings of this difficult area and the methods of help—still searching, still inquiring. In our over-all goal in helping, do we really want to make for likeness? In our changing society, generational differences are axiomatic. The aged person cannot be or act or feel like the adult child, nor can the adult child be or act or feel like the aged person. By acknowledging and using this need for difference, help to clients can be around their acceptance of each other's difference with the least amount of guilt possible rather than aiming to comfortingly cover and conceal the differences.

At this point Posner quotes from Herbert H. Aptekar to make his point in describing the situation where older adult and adult child come to a worker on the subject of placement of parent:

> Parent and child seldom see eye to eye on such a matter. There is conflict between them which must be resolved before the placement can ever be effected. In this type of situation, the worker becomes the focus of conflicting wills. Both persons who are at odds with each other, and who certainly have a different stake in the social service which is to be rendered by the agency, bring their conflict to the worker. He is the same worker, but what he has to offer is seen differently by the two persons directly involved. It would be possible to identify with one party to the conflict or with the other. The experienced and skilled worker who is dynamically oriented, however, will do neither. Both clients will project onto him their interests, thoughts, opinions and feelings. They bring their reactions to the service which he is able to render, and he can bring to them the real facts about placement which they need to know. He can tell them what he can do, recognizing that an important question is whether there can be any mutuality in their wanting it. How much together or how separate must they be in this? Can either move from his original position to see some of the outlook of the other? Can each one give in to the other sufficiently so that placement will become possible? Or must each hold on to the old view? The elderly person seldom looks for a profound change in his way of living. The younger person may often feel that he is being blocked by his elderly parent in his efforts to live differ-

ently. Each has a different outlook, a different goal to achieve, and the question is whether placement will enable them to achieve their respective goals. . . .[12]

Never is it enough for Posner that we understand, and then try to understand more. We must go on to let the people know that we do—by what we do. Just as he recognized the fears of the aged in approaching agencies for help and the reasons for the fear, so in relation to the adult child who comes to the agency with a problem around an older parent he saw a fear of condemnation, possibly a feeling of shame and guilt or a feeling of running counter to the traditions of the community. If the agency can show its full acceptance not merely of the adult child client as a person but of the implications of generational difference and the problems that come with it, if the agency by word and deed, through its very structure can show that it does not need to condemn, then the client's own condemnation of himself need not be so great either. For all concerned, agency acceptance must be the beginning of help.

Posner was one of the first in social work to seriously consider the generational component, anticipating and preparing the way for more recent explorations in this area.* One facet of it, however, seems uniquely Posner's. That was his including and studying the part played by the caseworker's own generation.

His concern began as a part of his pervasive concern that we social workers look at ourselves and know ourselves and continue to look again and to learn. At first he considered the caseworker as a person who had also had parents, a person perhaps with personal conflict in relation to her own parents. This she brings into her relationship with parents

---

*Perhaps most widely known is the thought of Margaret Blenkner in conceptualizing filial maturity. See her article "Social Work and Family Relationships in Later Life with Some Thought on Filial Maturity," *Social Structure and the Family: Generational Relations,* eds. Ethel Shanas and Gordon F. Streib (Englewood Cliffs: Prentice-Hall, 1964).

of others. Because her age is nearer to the adult child's age and because of her past experience, she will tend to identify with the adult child. Because she is so identified with the adult child, there may be guilt. Because of this, she may go all the way over to the old person's side without leaving room for the adult child's thinking and feeling. Or the case-worker who has had to take help in order to separate from her own parents may at times tend to identify with the adult child's problems, to see only separation as a solution and see any act of the adult child's going toward the parent in what might be a healthy relationship as a neurotic attach-ment. Whether or not the worker has a troubled bit of back-ground to influence either helping relationship, there is a more common problem to be considered. How does the worker herself feel about aging? Whatever the reaction, fearful or fearless, it has a part in the process and has its effect on the way we reach and speak and listen and act.

In later writings, Posner went beyond the fact that social workers carry left-over or current emotional effects of their own parental relationships, to the fact that the caseworker herself is a bearer of this generational component into the casework relationship.

By generational component, I mean first, that we deal with individuals who may be of different ages from each other and second, that we deal with diverse socio-cultural backgrounds, traditions, and values, which have at their base generational implications. In a child guidance situa-tion, there is the undeniable fact that we have a child and parent who are of different generations. We also have a caseworker who is of a different generation from the child and perhaps from the parent too.

In working with the aged, we are faced with the same phenomenon both in relation to the aged person and his adult child and in relation to the caseworker and the aged person, and in many instances in relation to the adult child. This, I suppose, is one of the dilemmas of casework. How can we help the child or any client, for that matter, who represents such great difference from us? . . . . How can we help an older person and his adult children in the face of their generational difference—their socio-cultural differences as well as our own?. . . . To understand more clearly the adult-child and older-adult parent relationship as seen from the perspective of the Jewish agency, I should like to represent it as a four dimensional entity consisting of agency, worker, adult child, and older parent, all interrelated with each other. I like to visualize it pictorially as a triangle with the worker at the apex, the adult child and older person representing each, one arm of the triangle, and the agency representing the lower connecting arm. . . . The caseworker is the pivotal point as well as the connecting link, with the agency on the one hand, and the adult child and older parent on the other. For one thing, the caseworker in a Jewish agency must possess some knowledge of the changes that have taken place in society with regard to the family as a whole, specifically the Jewish family, and the changed relationships with respect to the aged person in society and the family. These relationships are at variance with what has been described as the family relationship at the turn of the century when the older people of today grew up. It is important for the worker to know, too, that these changes in family living, although accepted by the second generation American Jew as valid for him, certainly may run counter to the socio-cultural attitudes of the first generation American Jew—the older person of today. Those of you who are familiar with the description of Jewish life in the old "shtetl," know what a different orientation some of the older people of today come from. The independence of the individual was safeguarded and in the eyes of the shtetl society an individual was no less a person because he needed help, or because he was old. These attitudes and traditions were brought over to this country in the various immigration waves of the latter part of the 19th and early part of the 20th centuries.

For the caseworker to have this knowledge as well as knowledge of religious practices, customs, and the chang-

ing patterns of family and community living gives him
some of the basic equipment required in his approach to
helping in generational conflict. It goes without saying
that this knowledge must consist also of a psychological
understanding of the meaning of the changes that have
taken place in America with regard to adult child and
older parent relationships.[13]

An individual is no less a person because he is aged.

10. *The Socio-cultural Factor.*

Although the socio-cultural has been enmeshed in the
above, it goes beyond just generational considerations and
stands by itself as one of the factors bearing wide influence
in the life of an aged person and the acceptance of all aged.
This may be especially true in current times when many of
our old people came here in mass immigrations bringing
another culture with them. And for those who were born
here time itself has provided sufficient changes in one life-
time to make American culture today something very different from that of the early 1900s. Those bred and tempered
in another time become aliens in their own land in this our
day of reverence for movement.

Always looking for weaknesses that once seen might be
altered, in one of his later articles Posner saw some pleasing
improvements in work with the aged, but only minimal
achievement in understanding their family complications.
This he felt was mainly due to another factor, one that had
received increasing attention in social work but which was
so easily ignored, namely the absence within thinking and
practice of an adequate socio-cultural underpinning as a
basic and inseparable part of casework practice with the
aged and their families. To him the socio-cultural included
the traditional or learned ways of behavior that become
established in social groups. Every individual makes them
part of his own way of life in relation to himself and the
group around him. More specifically, they covered the
knowledge, art, morals, law, customs, and habits acquired
by an individual as a member of a group or society.

Granting that socio-cultural factors had always played a part in the casework process, he felt they had been long undervalued. Because of the influences of psychiatry and psychoanalysis, casework was led to a denial of the importance of milieu. The great emphasis upon changing the individual had meant that socio-cultural elements rooted in tradition were seen as barriers to change. Instead of constraining factors Posner found differences within which individuals could achieve freedom and scope.

Considering studies made to evaluate the social and cultural changes that have occurred for older people as well as changes in the attitudes toward older people, he dwells upon some of the most pertinent developments:

> We have developed, according to David Riesman,[14] an "other-directed" society where the direction for most areas of living comes from others; from the outside; from our contemporaries; from our mass media. We learn to rear children from books; we eat what is advertised; we behave in fixed ways; and we are sensitive to how others look upon us. We have developed a conformity which is internalized for it is implanted early in our life and continues on throughout life. The parents of today, having grown up in a setting that was more "inner-directed," find at times a loss of old certainties; of self assurance in their role as parents.[15]

Because of this shift in authority from the parent to the expert, the parent of today may lose his self-esteem. In the past the ways of the grandparents were handed on to parent and then to child. Now a parent may find his traditional child-rearing methods questioned by outside experts.

At the same time, the American family has become a mobile family, constantly on the move, not establishing roots anywhere. With a great deal of emphasis upon the future, on goals to achieve, we have little patience with the past or with tradition. Also, with the urbanization of American life, there have been changes in housing, in recreation and in other areas of living that have tended to eliminate the grandparent from the home. While the child's parents try to keep up with the young, this cannot be done by the grandparent. He becomes a stranger within the circle of descendants.

Again Posner took a look at the profession, which always included a look at himself as a part of that profession. He believed social workers too often feared to give attention to many of the socio-cultural elements they met, particularly as they were related to their own background and traditions. But though we may fear or negate the differences older people represent insofar as American cultural tradition is concerned, unless there is some awareness of our client's cultural tradition, as well as our own, there will be the greatest difficulty in giving help. Thus he stressed the need for the caseworker to know himself culturally, and not to stop there:

> Although social workers may find it easy to talk about and to accept cultural relativity, that is, the difference that exists among groups or individuals, it is another matter when a person of a different culture comes for help and when we have to develop a close relationship with him. The attitude then is to consider him to be somewhat deviant and the temptation exists to reorient that person in line with our own cultural attitudes. It is difficult for us to accept emotionally that which may run counter to those attitudes that have become part of our own ego and superego structure, for this would represent a denial of ourselves. The culture conflict which results can often create innumerable difficulties in our work with clients. It may lead us at times to consider a cultural difference as an aberration of some sort or it may lead us to a treatment plan which runs counter to the client's own cultural orientation.[16]

In working with the aged more than with other groups, he found crucial importance in the background of the worker and the need for a sound consideration of those cultural accoutrements we carry. His emphasis on the worker's understanding of his own personality as shaped by his socio-cultural background was based upon his belief that therein lay the lead to an understanding of the dynamics of any casework relationship including that of the aged person and his adult child. An understanding of our own background would lead inevitably to a better understanding of the client's background. The result would be a meshing of the two toward real help.

11. *Potential.*

"Potential" may appear to be an incongruous conclusion to the items above if they have seemed to be a rather dreary collection. But they are not meant to be mainly negative. They are simply the reality factors to consider. This is what *might* happen when one is old. This is the way it *may* be. But it need not necessarily be always or even predominantly dreary. Posner may be upset with society and with social workers, but he has great faith in the older individual, and his belief in a capacity for growth is an integral part of everything he says. Any time the situation appears otherwise, it is to him a temporary inability to use inner strengths and capacities.

He reminds us that when we look for the distinguishing factors involved in simply being aged, there's sometimes the danger of attributing too much to age, digging out differences that have nothing to do with years. It is those who are unusual rather than those who are not who are most likely to come to and for the attention of the helping professions. The generic base of neurotic behavior may be the same for the old as for the young. The older person of today is the younger person of yesterday. There are older people who never become adults, who never cut the tie to their parents, who never establish a balance between dependence and independence.

For the most part, however, Posner's growing experience with older people and increasing understanding led him to see them as individuals, limited perhaps physically but within those limitations, able to move, change and grow. He denied the common belief that chronological age in and of itself lessened an older person's desire or ability for creativity.

As a result, one of his primary aims was to spread the word that casework with older persons is a valid process, that older people can make new adjustments and take responsibility for their living, that the dynamics inherent in the casework process can help both older persons and workers towards a philosophy of living rather than one of death.

Again, the internalizing of attitudes has been in action, and the blame goes back to attitudes, and the attitudes go back to the cultural values. The older person who thinks he has no potential most often has absorbed the thought from those around him. Caseworkers therefore have to assume the responsibility of seeing the person asking for help, regardless of his age, as a living person with rights, capacities, and a will. They need to acquire ever greater skills to discern the degree of a person's readiness and ability to involve his will, so that the client can come to use us to the limit of his ability.

And then, not only do we assume this ability to change but we work toward having the older person take as his own our more positive attitudes. Working with the older person's concept of time we can help him see it as a dynamic element of the present with life-giving properties rather than as an empty beginning of the end. Accepting the possibility of growth while there is yet life, the client can anticipate more steps of advancement in one way or another until faced with death in its proper place as the last step of life.

Notes

1. William Posner and Rochelle Indelman, "Jewish Community Services of Long Island—Manual of Policies and Procedures," March 1956, p. 4.

2. Grace Browning, "Social Services & the Aged," *The Family* (December 1936).

3. William Posner, "Characteristics of Casework with Older People —A Discussion of Basic Issues," National Committee on Aging Seminar, Harriman, 1960, p. 8.

4. ———, "Adapting and Sharpening Social Work Knowledge and Skills in Serving the Aged," *Social Work* (October 1957), p. 40.

5. ———, "Casework Process in a Private Residence Program for Older Persons," *Journal of Social Work Process* (May 1953), pp. 13–14.

6. William Posner and Rochelle Indelman, op. cit., pp. 25–26.

7. William Posner, "Casework Process in a Private Residence Program for Older Persons," op. cit., p. 12.

8. Ibid., p. 6.

9. William Posner and Arthur S. Farber, "Mrs. Benson Requests Placement," in *The Field of Social Work,* eds. Arthur E. Fink, Everett E. Wilson, Merrill B. Conover (New York: Henry Holt & Co., 1955).

10. William Posner, "Adapting and Sharpening Social Work Knowledge and Skills in Serving the Aged," op. cit., p. 40.

11. William Posner and Arthur S. Farber, op. cit., pp. 14–15.

12. Herbert H. Aptekar, *The Dynamics of Casework and Counseling* (Boston: Houghton Mifflin Co., 1955), pp. 85–86.

13. William Posner, "Socio-Cultural Factors in Casework with Adult Children and Aged Parents," *Journal of Jewish Communal Service* (Winter 1958), pp. 197–98.

14. David Riesman et al., *The Lonely Crowd* (New York: Doubleday Anchor, 1956).

15. William Posner, "Socio-Cultural Factors in Casework with Adult Children and Aged Parents," op. cit., p. 194.

16. Ibid., p. 199.

4

"LOVE IS CARING,
COMPELLED INTO ACTION"

. . . . . about agency action—policies and programs

ATTITUDES HAVE A PART in determining the types of services agencies give, but let us return to the continuum of need in work with the aging—attitudes, understanding, acceptance, and action—with the pliant linking and overlapping and circling back lines between the one and another portion of growth. In trying to present in order all that Posner had to contribute, there is much that will not lend itself to outline, that will not stay in one place but blends into another or pervades the whole. Understanding increases as attitudes change, but attitudes change, too, as understanding increases. "Acceptance" he defined as "accepting as valid" what we come to understand until the knowledge roots and lives within us. It grows from understanding, leads to action, and action has an effect on attitude.

But now, beyond the empathy and response that have been the focus so far, what of policies and very practical agency programs, the concrete evidence of just how much our attitudes and understanding and acceptance mean to us and to this center of our attention, the older client who needs help.

POLICY

What we do as individuals or agencies or communities or nations depends on what we believe. Aside from general social work values, Posner developed in his own thinking and his own agency some basic policies that he found necessary variations in working with older people. Each was new in the emphasis of his time. Each is still increasing in acceptance in our time.

1. *Specialization.*

Posner's view of the value of having agency departments devoted only to aging has been covered before as it influences the attitudes of workers and the growth of understanding. Here in agency practicalities, Posner saw it of great importance, too, where it concerned other staff aspects, such as recruiting, training, supervising. As mentioned before, for workers with all-inclusive caseloads in a family agency, the old had usually been left to the neglected last. With the general caseload arrangement it had been difficult to build enthusiasm and to do all that was thought necessary in developing workers knowledgeable on the subject of aging. From their experience with a separate department, the Long Island agency found staff getting more excited about the potentials and possibilities of caring for the old when their whole focus could be in the one area and when that area was given the recognition of a separate identity. Training of a small group of concentrated workers naturally became more practical and efficient.

In much the same way, the effectiveness of supervision increased. In the past, without a consistent focus, help from supervision in regard to a specific problem in family casework could not always be carried over to a case involving an elderly person, wanting and needing to cope with his problem in a different way than a younger person. Confusion resulted from administrative policies and procedures that could not be applied uniformly. Clarity and continuity came with the single-focus supervisory pattern of separation.

All of which naturally increased the effectiveness of service to the client. Posner was aware of the cons of specialization. At that time it was seen as a way of isolating one segment of people from another. Especially in family agencies this was considered in opposition to the favored way of giving to all who came the same kind of casework help. Although agreeing in theory, Posner saw the negative side far outweighed by the new levels of attention and understanding and aid given the older group who had never before really received equal emphasis.

2. *Individualization.*

Individualization for any human being was a part of Posner's creed, and we have looked at how it affected his explorations for understanding of older people, of each older person. Here it both stems from and leads to agency specialization. It was specialization that led him and his associates to the recognition that if help were really to be given, they had to see the older person as different from others. This difference, far from taking him out of the family group, actually helped them to understand him better. They could understand more clearly his position and role in the family and see him as someone who indeed had emotional strengths even though limited physically. So they began seeing the older client even more as an individual in his own right, able to respond to new situations and to adjust to them, and with the help of casework process to change and move forward.

Out of the recognition of individual strengths and resources and capacities for growth came an agency policy that focused not on doing *for* the older client, but on seeking ways in which he could do for himself, recognizing his ability to take responsibility even though in a limited way. As Posner's unfolding of the experience in his own agency continued, finer lines of discernment in the recognition of individual resources appeared. Because a person showed helplessness, caseworkers were inclined to think their full casework knowledge and skill were not applicable. Therefore they would accept the request, whatever it might be, at face value without seeking depth of individual need. Efforts to use the older person's capacities were blocked and caseworkers were not staying with the client long enough to get to the specifics of his problem, to a real knowledge of each different human being.

Even at best, some were unable to respond.

There are those who do have low thresholds and whose limitations are such that they are unable to participate in a casework process. To recognize these limitations in older persons is as essential as recognizing them in younger persons. I would be inclined to say, however, that I would be less fearful of overdoing than of underdoing; particularly if we ourselves can accept as valid that which is of greatest value for the client rather than what we think is good for him.[1]

Not what we would like to do or think is needed, but what would be of the most value to him—a fine distinction but a real one. Client-centered services, services as the client sees and wants and needs services, services based on the individual potential of each client—such services are unequivocably supported in page after page, year after year, by Posner. For every individual there were seen challenges imposed by the world, paradoxes of culture and economy, inner drives and outer stresses that required help in the balancing.

But in this field the ways of helping are more limited. More than for most clients, Posner saw much depending on the worker's earnest desire and ability to help the client find a way of drawing on his own individual inner strengths, strengths accumulated through the experience of many years. This he found crucial to growth, much more important than the popular use of outside stimulation. It is a part of his emphasis on the potential still alive in our last years. He sought strengths for being rather than for doing. The capacities for doing may decline; the growth of spirit may know no limit.

3. *Flexibility.*

Posner was a supervisor and an administrator, an agency man as well as a caseworker. Always alert to the need of new action following new understanding, his discernment went on to the meaning of a new action to old agency habits.

It never really seemed to be a question of where an agency might limit action, but always how the agency might adapt to the action presented by the understanding.

Looking at the physical and policy structure of his own agency and considering the way it must appear to an older client, he asked himself and his profession pertinent questions. Is the geographic location accessible for the older client with problems of transportation and stairways? Is the waiting room the kind that will reduce fears, the receptionist the kind to patiently dispel confusion? Are home visits allowed more freely for those who would have a major problem in coming to an office at a specified time? Are they allowed for the outreach to the ambivalent or reluctant client?

The questions covered minute details and philosophical approaches. They all asked in one way or another—are we willing to be flexible, to adapt and modify in order to meet need?

In his own agency the modifications were managed. Most of them involved time. In some cases, the agency pace was quickened. Phone calls were returned immediately or at the most within 24 hours. Appointments were set up with never more than a week's delay and emergency appointments were always available. Resulting action was taken as soon as possible. Waiting lists, believed unrealistic for older people whose time of life is limited, were eliminated.

Usually, however, flexibility of time meant more time, a slowing of the pace to the pace of the client. For the older person with the slower tempo of moving and reacting, caseloads allowed for more interviews, for longer interviews, for more home visits, for more time in working out adult children problems. And in spite of increasing emphasis on short-term help in other areas, more time was allowed over the full length of service. Taking into consideration the older person's low motivation and frequent confusion on how agencies work, the worker must take longer to reach out more. Repeated evidences of interest, support over an indefinite period of time were not only allowed but encouraged for Posner's staff. They knew the importance of one stable, continuing and reliable contact for the faltering and bewildered in an unstable world.

To be flexible, of course, meant to meet the need of the person in need as painlessly as possible—as fully as possible.

4. *Community Living.*

The adaptation, the outreach, all the agency programs instigated and supported by Posner had as a paramount aim the keeping of the individual in the community as long as possible. There he could have a life of his own, as much as possible a continuation of all that had given meaning to life. The first aim was to help a person find deeper and more secure roots within his family and the environment he had known.

It is not surprising, considering the emphasis placed on the capabilities of the older person when he is given an understanding approach with a positive attitude, that Posner was strongly opposed to our blanket use of institutions. Although he supported institutions for the many whose needs they met in the only possible way or for those who could develop best in such a milieu, he saw with gladness a moving away from the ideas of protection that had too long been held as the only answer. He acclaimed and helped promote ideas of care that were just beginning to grow based on individual need.

I should like to mention one other historical factor which has shaped or directed our thinking about the aged, and that is what has been called by many the "brick and mortar" concept. This concept is not, of course, the exclusive property of the aged field. It has been true in the past for the child care field as well. This view states that buildings have drama and appeal. They can be felt and seen. Those interested in them can visit the structures. They can be pointed out and, of course, you can raise money for them.

Psychologically, we can say that buildings satisfy our egos; we can see the fruits of our labor. In this self-satisfaction we give little heed to whether it is good for the client or resident. Fortunately, the attitudes of institutions are changing, too, but I mention this factor because I feel that in the aged field, anyway, it had for a long time militated against, sometimes overtly and sometimes unconsciously, the establishment of other forms of care.[2]

His views were based on the conviction that all people, young and old, belonged in the community unless they were so physically or mentally incapacitated that community living could constitute a danger to themselves or to others.

Few persons indeed will question this assumption for the so-called normal individual whether young or old. This is natural in view of the fact that ours has always been a family-oriented society and one that has cherished the freedom of the individual. This has not been as true, however, with regard to our attitude toward those who were considered as having deviated from the normal. In this respect our thinking has been largely institutional. It is only comparatively recently that the orphan asylum ceased to be the only resource for the care of the dependent and neglected child.

The home for the aged and nursing home are still the major agencies for the care of the aged and handicapped and the mental institution is still the number one resource for the mental patient.

Suffice it to say that the reasons for this type of institutional thinking relate to the internalization of stereotypes that have prevailed in our country about those who could not fend for themselves, who were more dependent than others, and who could not compete on the same level with others who were not burdened with handicaps.

Although we were ready to accept the individual differences of the so-called normal individual, we could not do so for the less fortunate; for them the answer was protection, isolation from others.[3]

So he saw the need for a wider acceptance of the value of community living in order to get to the next step of finding out what services were needed in order to keep older people in as normal a living situation as possible. Beyond recognizing the services needed he wanted consideration of what they were designed to do, how best to administer them, and how best to interpret them so that they would have meaning to the clients for whom they were intended as well as to the community that would be asked to support them.

Client-centered as always, the first question for Posner was, what is it that the client needs in order to stay where he is, and then what can we do about it? What have we done to the old or what has happened that brings them to the point of a need for some help in self-maintenance and how can we counteract it? One of the things we have done, of course, is become admirers of youth and advocates of speed. With youth orientation and changing philosophies of family service he found the emphasis of the time on counseling, on helping clients with relationship problems. Although this is helpful with many older clients, what they need, too, is help with living arrangements, with employment, with finances and health, with household help and transportation. Because of the woeful lack of community resources in such areas then—a lack we are as a nation far from filling now in spite of much progress—attempting to provide such services became a frustrating burden for the agencies and workers concentrating on the aged.

Money and health and housing and some care in order to stay in that housing, then, were the needs, and so were the easing of pain and loneliness and empty hours.

PROGRAMS

When we come to specific agency programs to support the policies and meet the needs, Posner spoke as the representative of his own agency, the Jewish Community Services of Long Island. It was an agency divided into three divisions: Services for Children, Family Services, and Services for the Aged. As the head of its Division for the Aging, and later as director of the entire organization, Posner had much to do with the services offered and the policies developed around the services. As their goals focused on keeping the client in the community, they found that this is what most older people really wanted, even though they were incapacitated by handicaps or chronic illness. And yet, their first request was most often for a home for the aged placement as they saw their ability to manage alone failing. They knew of no other possibility. What was surprising to Posner and his agency was that even after they had developed a variety of other services, the clients were suspicious. So entrenched had become the tradition of the home for aged as the only method of care that older people themselves began to look upon it as the ultimate end, even though to many it was threatening and not at all their own desire.

Although he wrote about the specific services of his agency in a number of articles, they are set forth most completely in the manual prepared for the staff, which departed somewhat from the traditional method of merely listing procedures and policies. It included much descriptive material of the casework process in order to make of procedures a two-way involvement. It elaborated on the psychological as well as the reality factors involved in each service to widen rather than circumscribe the horizons of practice.

There are 75 pages in this manual, and in outlining the services offered, my aim is to dwell mainly on Posner's perception of the dynamic and psychological factors involved in giving the service, with a brief description of the service itself. For those concerned with more process details, the two services he felt most important—the family residence and family aide services—are described in the Appendices. The services listed were different in kind and nature, but all had for their common goal the constructive purpose of strengthening life in the community. The goal of the services was to help people in times of personal crisis to use fully their own individual capacities and resources.

But even before a service was offered, some of the understanding of special factors applicable to older people had already been translated into action. Recalling one factor, for instance, age itself, the instructions to staff were explicit about taking care that the client felt as accepted as any younger or more competent client would, that he was helped to express his problem and to understand what the agency could do and what would be expected of him.

Another factor was time, and procedures outlined fit the policy discussed above.

Another was generations. Where intake was concerned, it was rare that the older person himself made the initial contact. He was almost always, however, considered the primary client. When it was the adult child or other responsible relative or friend who applied, the focus was centered mainly around the worker's responsibility to reach an understanding with the applicant as to the degree of his own involvement. This was done for the purpose of determining who really was the client. In such a situation the worker described the various services of the agency to enable the applicant to test his own reactions and choose the service which corresponded with his own feeling. An adult child could need individual counseling help for himself when the problem was only experienced by him, and in such a case the adult child would be the primary client.

However, when the applicant was able to see clearly that the problem came from a situation or emotional conflict related to an older person, the eligibility requirement of involving the older person was always stressed. While the weight of the problem might then be carried just as much and even more by the applicant rather than the older person, still the case would go under the name of the older person, thus making the older person the client. In this type of application, the continuation of the intake process would depend upon the applicant's readiness to involve the older person. As soon as this was accepted, the older person himself was required to communicate with the agency either by phone or letter to arrange his own appointment. Only in cases of extreme hardship and real inability by the older person to take this step would they permit someone else to do it for him.

This settled, and fees agreed upon—so to the services offered:

    1. *Family Aide Service.* (For agencies interested in establishing such a service, see complete details in Appendix B.)

This, known more commonly as homemaker service, is obviously aimed at community living, usually for the chronically ill person who cannot quite manage alone. Within his physical limitations, such a person was helped to organize his life with some feeling of independence and usefulness, or perhaps was aided to accept the inevitability of a need for change.

In any case time was considered a tool, whether as a means toward a different solution, for maintaining the client as he was, or for bringing him back to a state of self-sufficiency. Posner was seeking a realistic structure for service. A reality for the aged was that they did require more time, more time for recuperation, more time for decisions, more time for care.

Even so, in the beginning he favored setting up a definite time limit for any plan of helping. That was the way it was in other categories of need. Later he supported the extremely unpopular thought of permanent homemakers. Maximum time limits were eliminated even though this meant an administrative question on the value of tying up one homemaker on one case indefinitely. Would it mean a limitation of service to other clients in need of the same type of help? With sufficient funds to meet most such requests, his answer was found in the fact that unless a service is geared to the need of the client, there is little use in offering it. If the general proposition that older persons have slower recuperative powers is accepted, then so must there be different norms for judging time limitations, or lack of limitations, in the services provided.

Client-centered, need-focused—familiar themes by now; and there is that other continuing line of thought—that clients are individualized clients with individual needs, that there must be a differential use of the service. He emphasized again that the answer to need was not always doing "for." Although full-time Family Aide Service was usually required for acute illness, the aged were mainly people suffering from chronic conditions. He felt their ability to organize their lives well was not improved as much by a great deal of help as by regular and consistent assistance. By taking over only a few very basic necessary household chores, the family aide could make it possible for the elderly housewife to continue to manage by herself.

With older people there often comes a point of having few responsibilities for others. At the same time a good and proper caring for self may lose importance. When cooking for oneself has ceased to seem worthwhile to the client, the homemaker may find her most important role in bringing an undernourished worn-out person back to a normal state of strength.

When the Family Aide Service was used they sometimes found a different pattern of life developing in attitude and independence along with the return to the nourishment of regularity. Posner saw something else, too, in the times when the part-time help was not there. That was the psychological chance for clients to test themselves in the interims. Let it not be all a doing for; let them do and know themselves in the doing.

Homemaker service, or any service, was to Posner an opportunity for casework service, with the caseworker an integral part of a team including not only the homemaker but the doctor and various therapists as needed. It was the

caseworker who integrated and coordinated the service,
assuring the greatest value to the client. In discussing casework in homemaking he brings in quite clearly his view of
casework as a social work, leaving no doubt as to his opinion of its primary purpose in any area.

Defining homemaker service in this way, namely as a
casework service, has created considerable controversy.
There are those who feel that in many instances casework
service is not required. All the family wants, they say, is
the help of a person in the house. Why impose a battery
of casework services? What need is there to delve into
the client's personality? Doesn't this really scare people
away from the service?

Actually, as I see it from my own experience, these
questions are based upon a lack of understanding of the
meaning and use of casework service. It stems from a
tendency to view all of casework as a process which
delves deep into the psyche and is concerned only with
radical personality and psychological change. Although
there may be some who hold this view of casework, the
best service we can do to social work is to reject this
outright.

Casework is differential and based on individual need.
There will always be those families who will need intensive casework service, and homemaker service may very
well prove to be the vehicle through which this will be
given. There will be other families, however, who will
need only the warm understanding of a caseworker; a
caseworker who will utilize her skill only to recognize
what it means for a person to apply to a social agency
for help, to discuss eligibility requirements for the service,
to discuss payment for service and to help the client with
what to many may be a charity stigma, to consider with
the client and her family the meaning of having someone
come into the house to take over the client's accustomed
tasks and to give the family the reassurance that only a
responsible agency can give, to have someone who under-
stands what illness means to a client, and to interpret
that to the client and her family.

Continuing in this vein that ranges so widely around family aides, and deeply into the very fundamentals of social work:

> Part of the problem, of course, is with casework itself or with the caseworker who because of her training may find it far more difficult to understand these situations or those families who really have no personality problems and to use herself differently here than in other situations.

> What we must understand, then, with regard to the casework aspects of homemaker service, is first, that any community sponsored service must be given responsibly. By its very nature this must involve a responsible application process, a consideration of eligibility requirements, and a continued concern for the validity of the service. Secondly, if we can truly see the use of casework service as differential in nature, then the caseworker has the basic responsibility of determining how she is going to use herself with the client and what meaning this service has to the client. Third, it would seem to me that through casework we have the opportunity of seeing homemaker service as a family-oriented service. We cannot separate out the individual client and say that only she needs the agency's help. We know only too well that what affects one member of the family affects the others too.[4]

2. *Household Help.*

As is true of other agencies, there were two distinctions between "household help" or housekeepers, and "family aides" or homemakers.

One was that in the homemaker service, the agency employed the homemaker, trained and supervised her and assigned her to the proper case on the basis of her ability and capacity; in household help, the agency did not provide or employ the housekeeper, instead provided financial help to the client who then employed the housekeeper herself. The other distinction was that in household help, a client may be able to manage fairly well on her own and need help only with the heavy cleaning. In homemaker service the family's needs were more total with the homemaker doing the shopping, cooking, general cleaning, and some care of the patient.

Even though it was against general agency policy to offer more than one service at a time with the hope that the one service would result in such mobilization of the client's resources that he could face other problems independently, on occasion in the Services to the Aged division housekeeping help for heavy cleaning was allowed a client having continuing homemaker service. With the housekeeper situation, too, casework service was involved, and here, too, there was an allowance for flexibility on time. Help was allowed for long periods of time to older persons who could manage on their own but found it difficult to do the heavy housework. Providing assistance to employ a domestic often made the difference between living in relative comfort or discomfort. The psychological value of keeping one's home in good condition gave the older person a sense of continued independence and made the service an important one.

For Posner any service to a client in need of that service was important, and the intrinsic value of the service lay in its meaning to the client.

3. *Psychiatric Services.*

This was one area where a limitation of funds played a part in how much such service was allowed for treatment. Actual treatment was not commonly given but referral for diagnosis was made when symptoms appeared in a destructive degree with a wish for self-injury, or merely when there was a combination of such symptoms as incontinence without organic causes, disorganization in daily living, exaggerated suspiciousness, frequent crying or insomnia, compulsive cleanliness, or accumulation of very useless and old articles of clothing or furniture or some such.

As always, Posner looked for the effect of the problem on the people concerned. Ordinarily older people themselves

were not the ones to make a request for a psychiatric diagnosis or treatment. Usually family members applied because
they were at a loss to understand the changing behavior of
a parent. The agency found the family resistant to knowing
what was actually happening, a universal phenomenon
applying to families concerned about younger members as
well as older ones. Although the disturbed person rarely
applied for himself, as in all other aged services they
would at least see the person concerned even though they
were only able to get a picture of a completely confused
individual.

One of the most frequent situations requiring their psychiatric service was that involving senility. When families
were faced with the problem of a parent's senility, all their
fears, guilt, and anxiety became most pointed. The healthy
individuals could not grasp completely the implications of
deterioration and would much rather have faced seeing
their parent dead than living in another world. Then the
consciousness of such a wish created a most charged and
difficult feeling to live with.

Actual psychiatric treatment was not common, but such
situations led to the use of real counseling help and an
easing of the problem for all concerned.

4. *Employment Counseling.*

This service was offered around neither job placement
nor choice of work, but was seen as a valid service in relation to personal difficulties that the client was having on
the subject of working. Often a medical examination was
made a part of this in order to help the client have a more
realistic look at the possibilities. Depending on the individual, sometimes referral to employment services was made.
The personal conflict involved was the focus:

> On the one hand he may want to retire but feels un-
> comfortable about it. On the other hand, the one who
> really wants to be employed is faced with a discouraging

attitude on the part of the community. We can and we
believe we should, offer an older person counseling to
help him examine and work through his real motivation
for this request. For this purpose, we, as workers, have
to accept the natural ambivalence on the part of older
persons both to seek work as well as to wish not to work
any longer. Basically, it is only as we ourselves as workers
can see value in either choice, that we can feel free to
offer such a service. Both possibilities carry with them
something healthy and positive. Older persons have been
able to find employment and have been able to retire
constructively. . . . In other words, the client should gain
something psychologically from a contact with a worker,
so that his own personal resources are strengthened.
Such a situation should not be handled routinely, but
rather as a real counseling service. . . . For the client who
has to face realistically his own unemployability, either
because of the medical finding or his own psychological
attitude, a counseling service should reduce guilt about
such a decision.[5]

5. *Business Counseling and Business Loans.*

To give this rare service, the agency used the help of a
business consultant, and when loans appeared advisable,
another loan association.

The counseling service given was, as in all services, a
mutual clarification of the request, and personal help in
examining the client's real desires. With the element of risk
generating real fear and insecurity in the older person
wanting to venture into business or needing help in maintaining the one he had, there was a need for advice and
support. Also in view of the limited possibilities for employment rehabilitation for the older person, the agency felt
it was sound to expore the possibility of a small business as a means of an independent livelihood. At that time
little had been done in encouraging this in the general
community, but Posner saw a small business as possibly
permitting an older person to work to the extent of his

physical capacities. It could also lend itself to an individual and perhaps reduced work schedule more beneficial than a time-clock routine.

6. *Friendly Visiting.*

Performed by volunteers and case aides, Posner supported the reactivation of this service by community agencies for older clients in terms that left little doubt about the value he placed upon regular visiting by someone willing to establish a friendly contact. In their experience there were literally thousands of older persons who managed fairly well on their own but who needed only a person to visit them regularly, someone to go shopping with, someone they could look forward to seeing, someone who cared. Such older people might not need a specific professional service. All they wanted was a visitor, the establishment of a human contact, the feeling of still being counted as a human being.

For Posner's agency this always meant volunteers working under professional guidance. Under such guidance the dangers of over-protectiveness and excess sympathy were avoided and the service had tremendous emotional and psychological value for the older person as well as for the volunteer.

7. *Other Services.*

As must be already apparent, casework counseling was available to any older client around any subject. Referral to other resources was taken for granted when necessary. This included aid in bringing the fearful person to asking for financial assistance from the welfare department. In other ways, when money was not elsewhere available, the Services of the Aged managed interim financial assistance or, as in nursing home referrals, sometimes managed the difference between what one had and what one needed. Posner's staff had specific instructions on money giving and fee charging, but not without emphasis on the meaning of money to an older person and direction on keeping the psychological importance of waning resources in mind.

8. *Private Residence Program.*

As a finale of the specific services developed and promoted by Posner, this is the one that attracted his deepest devotion as he worked and spoke and wrote to establish it firmly in the thinking of social agencies. The service had been instituted a year before Posner went to Long Island and had been sanctioned for that agency by the Jewish Federation on a city-wide basis, making it distinct from other services offered for community only. Posner brought his experience in child foster-home placement and his dedication to the philosophy of keeping older people in the community and put them to work in expanding the service and enhancing the casework involved. For along with its practical aspects, it was equally a casework service designed for those emotionally ready to become involved with a worker around a helping process.

Whereas all other services (with the exception of referrals to nursing homes) were intended to keep the client in his home or with his family, this one meant separation from the familiar. Posner realized the trauma involved, the resistances to the threat of agency supervision cr residence regulations, and felt there must be continuing supportive and clarifying counsel. Essentially, this type of placement was made available only to those who could utilize their strengths in it. They did not require as a condition of placement the client's total subservience to agency or home. They did not control his coming or going or require him to give up his friends or the treasured possessions he might want to bring with him into the home. Similarly beyond the initial and continued verification of income, the agency did not require the client to "sign over" everything to the agency. And always he had the choice of either remaining in placement or leaving it.

With such help, the service was aimed at the person who

could no longer manage alone, even with homemaker help. For this person, and especially the blind, the handicapped, the person on discharge from a mental hospital, there was then no alternative but an institution. Seeing this as an insufficient answer for the comparatively well person, in the beginning the agency sought substitute homes for the older person. With his usual clarity of evaluation, Posner found that this was more idealistic than realistic. Few older applicants requested a real substitute family home. They did not approach placement with a view of developing close ties with the comparatively strange home. Nor did the residence owners feel ready to give themselves completely to a comparative stranger.

Thus the agency arrived at the realization that the selection of a home had to be geared to the use that the client intended to make of it. It became clear that the nature of the placement process was such that it was really difficult to help a person in times of such personal crisis to evaluate his specific needs in the area of relationships. What he needed was help in reaching a decision to take such a step.

Recognizing that it was impossible in the placement process to get a full picture of the clients' relationships, and looking generally for homes where there was sensitivity and warmth toward older people, they came to see the "residence" as a place where a person resides with a family that undertakes to assist him to function to the maximum of his capacities. With this as a base there was the recognition that each residence was able to help in their particular way and could only meet the needs of those clients who could adjust to that way of living. Residences were of many types. So were the older persons. Therefore, the feelings, values, needs, and desires of both resident and residence were evaluated in making placements. Whether or not it worked for mutual benefit depended largely on evolving relationships and the freedom with which both client and residence owner could be themselves together. Both client and residence owner had to retain their difference. The aim of placement was not for a total personality change, either on the part of the older client or residence owner, but for adjustment of that part of each self which enabled them to use each other for continued living.

Appendix C gives a comprehensive description of the placement process, especially as it concerns the client and the caseworker and the residence owner in their relationships and interaction, in order to make of the placement a constructive experience for all concerned. Since it rather briefly sets forth the original requirements for eligibility of residences, some of the dynamics involved as given in the staff manual are added here. Of course, the residence owner, too, was considered as an individual with strengths and needs:

> The casework dynamics of the residence finding process has developed around our philosophy of the residence's relationship with the agency. In contrast to the residence owner's other relationships, be it with family or boarders, the agency emerges for him as a community source for help. Frequently it is the first encounter of the residence owner with a social agency, and like a client, the residence family meets with it in a very uncertain manner. On the one hand, many people welcome it, but on the other hand, some see a loss of independence in having applied to an agency. . . . The workers have to be able to help him find the balance between some relationship with the agency and the retaining of his own way of living. . . . The agency is always here to help. . . .[6]

Posner goes on, in detailing the eligibility requirements, to help his staff to sense from the reactions of the residence owners to some of the requirements, their real feelings for and potential adaptability to older people. Occasionally he dwells longer on particularly pertinent matters. Food, for instance, is one of the main concerns of older persons of comparative inactivity and dulled sense of taste. What they need and what they want and what the residence owner serves often combine into an area of conflict:

Frequently, however, we see that the food conflict is only an expression of another one between the residence owner and resident, and here is where the worker has to use his diagnostic understanding. When a resident expresses dissatisfaction with the quality of the food, or quantity, or the way it is served, is he really basing it on reality or is he asking for something else? A person craving a lot of attention or sympathy may make unreasonable demands for unusual foods. A very sick person who does not want to face his illness may disregard it completely by demanding most harmful foods. A residence owner may often express a punitive attitude by completely disregarding a resident's food preference.[7]

Although not a matter of rule, Posner looked for the psychological implications where a resident owner chose not to eat with the resident or chose to serve different foods to self and family than to resident. These things might be allowed but would certainly be explored, and in any case they asked that meals be prepared tastefully, that menus be varied, that food be served aesthetically—above all that the client be served "patiently and givingly."

As for attention during illness, assistance during acute illness and necessary home care was a definite requirement —for psychological as well as physical reasons. Posner stressed that no human being could feel like one without knowing that someone will care for him in illness, as well as in health. Their whole philosophy of placement—to prolong one's life in the community for as long as possible— seems to have been expressed in this requirement. If an older person has no one to take care of him in illness, he may become extremely fearful of his future and ability to continue to live in the community. Recuperating at home adds motivation for the effort to improve and remain where he is.

Aiming for this life in the community, for anything possible that would be conducive to a satisfactory life, and for residences ready to give as well as take, Posner did not see the listed eligibility requirements as being all inclusive. For placement involved a total living experience encompassing many facets as unpredictable as life itself. Imagination, flexibility and sensitive interpretation were caseworker requirements.

Placement meant above all a continuation, not a suspension of living.

9. *Relationship.*

Imagination and flexibility and sensitive interpretation were essential ingredients, too, in the caseworker's use of self in every case. Relationship might seem better placed with the policy guidelines above, but for Posner it was a specific service in itself although applicable in all other ways of service.

Throughout the exploration of attitude and understanding and acceptance, and culminating in the outlines for action, came a call for willingness and freedom to use and give of oneself in working with older people. Granted that this is an ideal part of all casework, here it seemed to Posner so especially important that he saw it as the only route for accomplishing anything in the way of service with the aged. Along with his belief in the dignity and worth of the individual, he added the "sacredness" of the casework relationship.

This has been either mentioned or taken for granted in previous quotations, but to focus on it for a moment, it was the essence of all he said about people, and for him the essence of this sacred relationship was, I think, stated simply and succinctly in two words used in a case description—"we together." For these older people who have known many losses, much rejection, who are often bewildered and alone, the worker must convey a genuine and heartfelt giving—in the beginning, along the way, and during the ending of the casework process.

"We together," and yet he did not mean to stray from a constructive and professional objectivity—compassion, yes, but also clarity of thinking. Posner knew the need for continuous professional development based upon a greater self-awareness was recognized in all fields of social work. He was aware of the emphasis on professional discipline and development stressed from the first day of a student's contact with a school of social work, and saw it as continuous throughout his progress as a worker, through all stages of his professional life. Any worker is called upon to grow by assimilating changes from without and within. Social work is not an easy profession, Posner commented, since the worker's constructive and positive involvement of his own "self" is continuously called upon. He was convinced that in working with the aged, there could be little restraint in a willingness to share of self or there would be little accomplished.

We have already dwelt upon the need to look at one's own age and culture and the client's age and culture as essential to understanding; we return to these aspects here as they involve not only understanding but also the way the worker goes on to use this understanding in the way he uses himself in the sacred relationship.

The "we together" of client and caseworker may encompass different ideas of help. In such case the effectiveness of the ongoing process would depend upon an aware and flexible use of the agency's function and structure. Posner knew there was no formula to be given as to the actual way an interview should be conducted. He stressed, however, the fact that the worker must be aware always of his responsibility toward the client and of the difference between the caseworker's conception of what constitutes help and the client's. While he warned against a misuse of service, on the other hand he felt the worker had to be able to distinguish between misuse of service and the struggle that goes on around the use of it. No two individuals use a service the same way. No two individuals react to their difficulties the same way. Nor do any two caseworkers offer service and selves identically.

So, in giving generously, in offering ourselves freely for a closer relationship than may be helpful in other categories, still for Posner it had to be with an aware use of self, and with a continuing acknowledgment of the client.

In working with older people, it is extremely important to evaluate (wherever possible on a conscious level with the client himself) whether the client uses the service for its specific purpose, or whether he uses it for the opportunity it offers for a close relationship with a younger person. The social worker may be used by the client for a personal attachment, as a link to the outside world. The older person's ties with his own family may have lessened, or he may have lost his close friends. The contact with a younger person may thus bring back vividly the older person's past through a reminiscence of his own vigorous young years. While this might be helpful, it is not the agency's function to serve this purpose. The worker cannot serve as a substitute for all the lost emotions and experiences. The worker's helpfulness flows from his ability to identify with the agency's function. This serves to establish the difference between professional help and friendly companionship. The reality of agency must be present in order that help be effective.[8]

Such evaluation of the client's use of service and the worker's use of self is a continuing part of the professional's ongoing process, and as must be already apparent, it should not be a light look but a deep and searching scrutiny of what is needed, what's happening, and what might be improved. It must be a scrutiny that neither rationalizes nor denies the worker's or the agency's faults and failures.

Concerning both relationship and evaluation, Posner speaks of the importance of the closing phase of casework process as an area that needs much more attention. To him a completed experience was of utmost importance, and no matter what the reasons for termination of contract might be, he wanted them discussed. The discussion was to include an assumption of responsibility for mistakes by the worker, as well as a classification of the client's responsibilities at the time of ending. Ideally, the ending process would take place in an atmosphere of freedom and comfort for the client, and would in itself become a true helping service, paving the way for a client to better mobilize his own resources thereafter and to continue growth.

The ending of a relationship comes and Posner looks at the whole of the relationship not only as the opportunity to give, but the chance to gain, for it will have been one of mutual value. The worker will have an arena for working through his own feelings about his own aging, and in many instances will find a personal enrichment from inspirational examples.

Those of us who have been in casework practice with the aged need no justification of its validity and of its great value. Our day-to-day experience gives ample proof of that. It is our hope that others of our profession, who have not had this experience or who have resisted it, will consider the great potentials of this area of service. For in it lies not only the promise of help to a large segment of our population, but the promise of personal growth for the caseworker.[9]

Notes

1. William Posner, "New Horizons in Casework with the Aged," Welfare and Health Council of New York City, March 1955, p. 9.

2. ————, "Meeting the Needs of the Aged in the Community," Council of Jewish Federations and Welfare Funds, Atlantic City, March 1953, p. 2.

3. ————, "A Case History of the Development of Non-Institutional Services for the Aged," Florida Council on Aging, Tampa, May 1958, p. 6.

4. ————, "Fulfilling Homemaking and Housekeeping Needs," Pittsburgh Bicentennial, May 1959, p. 28.

5. William Posner and Rochelle Indelman, "Jewish Community Services of Long Island—Manual of Policies and Procedures in the Division of Services for the Aged," March 1956, p. 32.

6. Ibid., p. 64.

7. Ibid., p. 68.

8. Ibid., p. 15.

9. William Posner, "Casework with the Aged: Challenge or Retreat," *American Journal of Orthopsychiatry* (April 1958), p. 333. © The American Orthopsychiatric Society, Inc. Reproduced with permission.

5

"STIRRINGS"

. . . . . about action in the field and community

> *the ultimate test of progress . . . must be seen*
> *in the stirrings and in the impatience that*
> *communities and agencies present. . . .*[1]

FOR MORE UNDERSTANDING, more skill, more qualified and
caring workers in the area of the aged, Posner dedicated his
life—certainly in the filling of his days, perhaps in the
numbering of them. Beyond his own work and his own
development and his own agency, he went into the subject
of aging in breadth and length and depth. He went back
into history. He dug deeply into a soul-searching of self
and profession and society. He took the cause of the aging
beyond social work to share and to coordinate with other
professions.

He went out to spread the word in the community. Always
he looked ahead.

DEPTH WITHIN THE PROFESSION

Posner had written articles and made speeches before,
but it was his experience with the new foster home possibilities for the aging that led him to an expansion of these
talents as he went forth when called upon within the social
work profession to explain and inspire. As his own experience and thinking developed, so did the content of the talks
and the written words, and so did his reputation grow to
that point of being nationally considered an expert and a
leader, within and without social work circles, where the
subject of aging was concerned.

Reading the articles in chronological order, it is interesting to note some of the changing views of how much had

been accomplished and what was needed. Never, however, was there any real change in the intensity of his view of the magnitude of the need, or a decrease in impatience at the pace of the progress.

In 1949 after a year with the Long Island agency, he made his first speech on the merits of the private residence program. By that time he was already Chairman of the Conference Group on Welfare of the Aged, a part of the Welfare Council of New York, and as such began what became a long journey with other professions into community action by presenting a paper on New York City's work with the elderly. At this time there was some optimism:

> It has become rather customary, in this complex society in which we live, to speak with gloom about the many social problems that face us and the difficulties that stand in the way of their solution. The problems of the elderly are indeed no exception to this rule. That the elderly are fast becoming our number one social problem is all too clear to informed persons everywhere. Perhaps fewer persons are aware of the difficulties inherent in the resolution of those problems. It would be only fair to say . . . that even in this regard the past few years have seen a crescendo of activity—at least in the social welfare and medical fields—in behalf of the older person, and real efforts have been made to recognize and cope with the many aspects of the situation.
>
> Without wishing to minimize the seriousness of the problems facing the elderly, nor to underestimate the tasks lying ahead, I should like to deviate somewhat from the accepted rule and present a picture of creative activity and accomplishment in behalf of the aged.[2]

He does that, describing advances in dissemination of information, raising standards of homes for the aged, providing some housing, some recreation, some increased medical facilities, and concludes that it was all very exciting and yet had only scratched the surface.

Three years later, speaking to the Welfare and Health

Council of New York City, there was a more pessimistic attitude and the restlessness showed. He had been involved for several years now. Change there had been, but not enough. Looking back over the past decade, as he had been asked to do, did not fill him with any desire to go back to those "good old days." Acknowledging the negative note as a personal bias, he described it as rooted in a feeling of impatience at the little that had as yet been done.

At that time he saw some small progress. More and more older people were coming to social agencies and some policy changes had been made. Because of the conviction of a small group of social workers who had demonstrated that the principles of casework and counseling applied to older persons as they did to others, agencies and social workers were beginning to have a better acceptance of giving help to older persons.

Three years after that—in 1955—he was giving tribute to those few social workers involved with the aged, and to their dedicated spirit in conveying to others that simple truth that aged people are important. Presenting the views of a study group on casework with the aged to the Welfare and Health Council of New York City, his words show a move toward integrating social work and community aims with a goal of more effective service for each one individual older client. He spoke of American social work theory as being closely associated with the free institutions of a democratic society. He wanted his audience to see the tie between the basic tenets of American social work and our religious, cultural and political heritage—alike in principles about the dignity of the individual, the acceptance of the individual, the free choice of the individual.

Perhaps through working with the study group involving other disciplines, he found a less rosy picture of much real social work progress. Instead there were the same perplexing questions that he had begun asking when he himself began his involvement with the aged—why had casework with aged received less attention in social work than other fields? Why had so few services and facilities been developed? Why had the aged received so little attention in family agencies, in hospitals, in employment agencies and in religious institutions? Why don't we seem to care?

In 1957, addressing social workers throughout the nation in their *Social Work* magazine, he acknowledged an increase in popular concern and interest, but was asking— what has social work done? Were we keeping pace with the others in advancing?

Aging as a community concern has become respectable. Not a day passes without seeing a newspaper or magazine article which emphasizes those problems associated with aging, such as retirement, employment, health, social and psychological relationships. During this last year alone, at least ten writers have interviewed this author, eager to get onto the profitable bandwagon. This is a heartening advance, considering that only a few short years ago it was hard to get even so much as a notice in the local press informing the public of the existence of the welfare council's hobby show for older persons.

On the face of it, then, there has been a real change in the community's concerns about the aging. The logical question that follows is: What has this growing concern done to professional thinking and practice? Has there been a similar advance in theory and in techniques of helping?

Primarily concerned as we are with social work thinking and practice, have we kept pace with the times, so to speak? Do we in social work have a better understanding of aging today than we did two decades ago or even one decade ago? Do we know more about what has been called the aging process—the physiological and psychological aspects of this process? And in the specific areas of social work, what new developments have taken place in casework—in helping the individual aging person in group work, in research, in community organization, in professional education?[3]

He acknowledged the answers were neither clear nor complete but from his own view of what had been happening in social work, the developments had been uneven and the sum total was little indeed. It compared in neither quality nor quantity with the progress in other fields.

Looking at education and · casework and research, he found nothing of much consequence. Looking at group work and community organization there was a glimmer of light. Group work agencies did have programs for the aging and were making some significant contributions in terms of technique and practice. Also many communities were studying the needs of the aged, and doing concrete social planning for the future. Even though some of the surveys stopped at the planning stage, still there was visible ferment. And he looked at public agencies, long aware of the problems of older people quantitatively if not qualitatively, and saw legislative and executive committees and commissions in many states concerned with the problems and involving social work in their search for answers.

So he found some positives in the general picture.

> But let us get down to people—to the individual client who is the object of concern. Our task as social workers, no matter in what area we work or in which functional field our interest lies, is to help the individual client— the individual older person and his family—but it is here, in this very spot, that a great problem exists. There is a vast difference between being concerned with a problem and doing something about it; although the object of our concern has been the aged in general, somehow we have not really been able to do much thus far for the individual older person who comes to us for help. . . .[4]

A thought of the spiralling cycle returns. Wherever we enter it, attitude without action is not enough.

BREADTH BETWEEN PROFESSIONS

The following year, Posner took his social work confession to share with other professions at the Orthopsy-

chiatry meeting and in the pages of their publication. He
was elated at their having a workshop on "Changing Concepts in Care of the Aged," but granted that the title of his
own paper—"Casework with the Aged: Challenge or Retreat"—had in it an element of anger. Nearly ten years
after his first expression of dismay at how little challenge
family agencies and caseworkers found in working with
the aged, his interim experience had only brought him to
this point of expressing the same dismay with more authority to a wider audience. It was a lack of challenge that he
found applicable not only to the old but to the chronically
ill and other hard-to-reach areas where goals could not
include quick and obvious accomplishment.

For such situations, the concern was there in the family
agency. An awareness of the problem was there. But in
agencies traditionally known as the place for anyone to turn
for help, the pace in developing new knowledge and skill
had not begun to keep up with the growing concern about
the growing problems of older people.

He found this not too surprising considering the transformation of the family agency into an "acute" agency,
trying perhaps to imitate developments in the medical field
by emphasizing the dramatic, the changes that could be
accomplished in short periods of time, forgetting that there
are those who need longer periods of care and service. Or,
he asked, was it a reaction to the period when family agencies literally controlled the lives of their clients over many
years? Whatever the cause, he saw an explosion of interest
and knowledge around the aged in other fields, and he saw
a standing still in social work.

In this paper, for this inter-disciplinary gathering, Posner
reached out in breadth, not just to deplore some aspects
but also for making clear some strengths. He told them
about family agencies and at the same time that there was
breadth, there was length, he took a long view—back:

> Perhaps we lack today the necessary historical perspec-
> tive of the family agency, its evolution through the years,
> its adaptation and changes with changing times and the

changing needs of people. . . . The function and scope of the family agency and its family-oriented philosophy have never excluded specific family members from its concern. . . . Its belief in people has historically never been based upon a policy of exclusiveness, but rather upon one which has recognized the needs of all people regardless of age or condition.

By its very definition . . . a family agency is concerned with the whole family, with its individual members, with their relationship to each other and with the totality of the family unit itself. The family agency is concerned with family preservation. Its whole philosophy and practice is thus family-oriented. To this extent family agency philosophy and practice may represent a uniqueness when compared with other helping disciplines, for we are as concerned in the area of chronic illness, for example, with what happens to the spouse and children of a long-term patient as we are with the patient himself. The client and his family are both our equal concern. [Our role is] helping not only the chronically ill or long term patient accept his own situation, but in helping him and his family to adjust to each other in the changed circumstances. . . . Our concern, too, is with the changes that take place in feelings of self-worth, in changed occupational and sex relationships. . . . In a situation involving the chronically ill, all family members may need help.[5]

It was a good review of the family agency contribution that he gave to the other professions, but then the confession began as he explained the connection between the historical review he had made and the present situation. From a heritage of granting an all-encompassing service to a family, the path to the present had strayed to a point of granting a far from all-encompassing family service—at least as far as the aged client was concerned.

Length in Looking Back at History

In a number of places such as the meeting just mentioned, Posner brought bits of history—of social work, casework,

Jewish agencies, particular services—always in a way that seemed a looking back in order to see where they had come from and where they were going. It was not just questioning what had been done and was being done and should be done, but why. It was not just a factual look back but a search for growth, or as in the example just above, blocks to growth.

These were just glimpses, however, compared to the scholarly research he did into the literature of the past on casework with the aged for a position paper on casework prepared for a seminar on aging conducted by the Council on Social Work Education in Aspen in 1958.[6] Here he set himself to reviewing the writing of the previous 40 years, a period of time that included the beginning of casework and its development as a vital and significant form of helping, in order to see how developments had affected understanding and work with the aged. This was to him a necessary prerequisite to any understanding of their present knowledge of the subject. Full awareness of present knowledge was a necessary prerequisite for thoughts on future directions in teaching and helping.

Although he regretted the study could not be even more exhaustive, it was indeed a full one (the bibliography listed 113 references) bringing out the developments of casework with the aged from the time when there was none to the year of 1958 when there was much and still much need for more. Even in the first decades of the twentieth century the American people began to see old age as a special problem, directing their attention toward the improvement of the condition of retired and disabled older workers living in poverty and misery in poorhouses and other types of institutions. The first full length general article on problems of the aged Posner found was in 1926. It described the differences between the modern and the old family pointing out that the large family of the past had been organized in the interests of the older generation to resist change and to perpetuate the family pattern.[7]

The possible applications of casework were first noted later in 1926. Already at that time workers were aware of the reluctance of the aged to seek help, but the help given by charity organizations was aimed only at the "helpable," leaving the chronically ill and those who could not be expected to become self-supporting to the care of the Poor Law or an almshouse. It was, eventually, the shortage of institutional beds that forced a more special attention to older people. Social work began to see a need for real imagination and ingenuity in the use of casework skill for the essential differences of human beings.

Marking the points of progress he saw as most pertinent, Posner described at length an article about Francis Bardwell, pioneer in the field, who saw the deficiencies of the time and looked ahead. The article stressed the point that workers in the field had to see the benefit and welfare of the aged individual as their first consideration. This meant loving old people, having confidence in them. It meant helping the impossible client. It meant meeting the older person on his own ground. It hopefully meant a future with adequate provision for the aged sick, industries for the limited, trained workers for all.[8]

Mr. Bardwell was indeed a pioneer. Later, in 1930, he was a speaker at the Chicago Conference on Care of the Aged, one of the first such large scale conferences, with perhaps the beginnings of the crusade Posner was later to assume on his own. Here he spoke of the importance of sound investigation of applicants for institutional admission, the importance of help to the nearly dependent in order to prevent institutionalization, and the urgent need of friendly visitors.[9]

In the 1930's casework itself went through considerable soul-searching and evaluation, partly triggered by Virginia Robinson's revolutionary emphasis on the casework relationship between client and worker as basic to helping, to bringing caseworkers to a greater awareness of the client as a person, and to a greater acceptance of the client's role in the helping relationship.[10] It was also the decade of the depression. Is it incidental that social work began to turn its attention from the sick and pathological toward seeing the strengths and potential and normalcy of people? A theme dear to Posner, he quotes from a 1936 *Family* article that stressed how important it is not to take away the older person's independence:

> In a world lamentably short of complete civilization we should not ignore—even temporarily—the possible ways of real social usefulness of the competent older person. . . . The dynamic still existing in a person in the old age group is an asset or a liability to be reckoned with and one whose outlets may be bettered with the help and the thinking and insight of a caseworker. The social view of this dynamic is something that needs to find its way into the bones and nerves of people; it requires a change in the inbred folk traditions of our time.[11]

At this time in the middle of the depression when quantity rather than quality was the order of the day, Grace Browning wrote an article with a special plea in behalf of casework for the aged and Posner found it a significant turning point in general thinking. Miss Browning asked the kind of probing questions Posner himself favored. She sought answers on the benefits of professional help. She looked at the fears and conflicts and confusions and found a clear need for trained workers who would have a skill in interviewing, a knowledge of the social aspects of degenerative diseases, an ability to become interested in each individual and enter into relationships, and that rarely mentioned ingredient, a love for old people.[12]

It was a turning point year, too, in that in it the Family Welfare Association of America set up an informal conference on the problems of the aged in order to gather together record material, adding to more understanding and more caring, more science. Commenting on this group in 1938, a *Family* editorial pointed out that the stress had been on what is common about old age rather than what is different —the different older persons with different backgrounds and different personalities:

> The social casework problem is to help old people accept their own reality. . . . The degree of limitation of the aged individual can only be measured against what he has done in more active periods. What he can or cannot do can be measured not against other old persons of the same age but only against his earlier self.[13]

For the decade of the '40s the emphasis on individualizing continued with a valiant effort on the part of some social workers to go beyond generic principles to describe specific processes and specific services. What do we *do* with relative responsibility laws? What do we *do* about parent-adult child relationships? How do we treat the psychological implications of aging problems? Yet others in the late '40s, even as Posner, found it necessary to remind social workers and social agencies that they were still not sufficiently sensitive to the problems of the aging client coming for help.

> We project our own rejection of old age and it blocks our ability to help. We rely too much on palliative measures and we don't even attempt to search out a person's fears and anxieties. We push him into a groove and we think we are making the older person comfortable when in reality we make ourselves comfortable. Older years have meaning; no life is complete without it. Unless we are able to respond to the older person's reaching out to us we shall be unable to help.[14]

Others also considered the advantages of specialized service for development of knowledge, increase of skills, and avoiding the necessity for competing with younger clients. In this time Posner saw the growing needs of older persons on the one hand clamoring for attention, and on the other, the continuing struggle within the family agency

field over starting specialized services that might run counter
to the accepted generic base.

The period from 1950 to 1958 was seen as the most productive in the development of casework services for the
aged, a development that received great impetus on a
national level from the first National Conference on Aging
called in 1950 by the Federal Security Agency. In Posner's
own geographical area at about the same time there was a
similar impact made by the New York State Joint Legislative Committee on Problems of the Aging, the first official
state group to be concerned. He mentions other evidences
of the growth of activities in other disciplines—e.g., the
founding of the Gerontological Society and the American
Geriatrics Society—and saw a tremendous growth of concern about the aging building up in the community as a
whole. However, although there was some movement in
social work, again he found it surprising that the crescendo
of activity in other disciplines, in communities and govern-
ment agencies, was not reflected to the same extent in his
own profession.

Often casework literature reflected thinking of psychiatrists on personality development in aging. Many of the
articles published represented the results of psychiatrists'
activity in homes for the aged and state hospitals. Development in the institutional area was one of the highlights of
the '50s. At least here the growing impact of trained social
workers had led to a new kind of thinking on institutional
placement.

Finally, he saw this period as a time of beginning to make
up for the general lack of case material for teaching pur-
poses, pointing up the greater concern that teachers as well
as practitioners were showing with respect to this aged
group, pointing gladly to the profession's new quest for new
attitudes, new methods and new processes.

The preparation for this paper at the Aspen Conference
was not only a huge undertaking, but it resulted in a per-
ceptible change of tone in the things he said later. Typically,
he readily stated the humbling effect of the work:

   I cannot refrain from commenting that as I became
more and more immersed in the literature, I began to
change some of my previous views about the amount of
material available on casework with the aged, as well as
about the quality of this ˙material. I had always com-
plained about the paucity of material and the comparative
lack of creativity in this area. . . . While it is true that
other specialized areas have a longer history and thus
have had wider and more intensive discussion, I am thor-
oughly convinced at this time, as I see the material in
perspective, that considering the aged field's slow start,
tremendous headway has been made, particularly during
the past decade.[15]

The looking back had a strengthening effect, too, and his
later writings had a more confident quality somehow, as if
he had found it encouraging to see that in all his deepest
convictions and what had sometimes seemed to be futile
efforts, he had not, after all, been all alone.

COLLABORATION IN COMMUNITY

At the same time Posner was getting a new perspective
on the contributions of others in the professions, his activities
beyond the profession increased culminating in the White
House Conference of 1961, for which he was a consultant.
Before it convened however, as a member of the New York
State Welfare Conference, he prepared an analysis of the
New York State Recommendations for the Conference. It
was an exciting business for him, seeing the involvement of
2500 persons from all walks of life in the preparatory
meetings.
The two years of preparation for the Conference became
an intensive community effort, reaching into virtually every
city, county, town, and village. The subject of aging over
this period found its way into the agenda of the national,
state, and local conferences of business, labor, health, welfare, and religious groups. Fraternal organizations, associa-
tions for the advancement of science and education, university and library groups, housing organizations—all became

interested in considering the implications of aging for their work and programs. The pre-conference preparations and discussions brought issues to the forefront. Being part of a nationwide effort meant seeing the issues not merely in their general framework, but specifically, as they related to different parts of the country, to large and small communities, to rural and urban areas. It was indeed an enthralling culmination to years of concern.

The same element of being impressed and perhaps surprised by the extent of the concern of all kinds of people is found in his report on the conference after it was held. At least he was impressed with the interest and the recommendations. He still awaited the putting of words into action. Still, this man who had taken over a special department for older people in 1949, who had later found comrades-in-arms within his profession, now knew without doubt that neither he nor his profession had a monopoly of concern in the field. It must have been a matter of comfort, a reason for rejoicing—and yet:

"We are only at the threshold. . . ."

Notes

1. William Posner, "Meeting the Needs of the Aged in the Community," Council of Jewish Federations and Welfare Funds, March 1953, p. 1.

2. ———, "New York City's Work with the Elderly," Legislative Document #12, Joint Legislative Committee on Problems of the Aging, 1950, p. 4.

3. ———, "Adapting and Sharpening Social Work Knowledge and Skills in Serving the Aged," *Social Work* II, no. 4 (October 1957), p. 37.

4. Ibid., p. 38.

5. ———, "Casework with the Aged: Challenge or Retreat," *American Journal of Orthopsychiatry* XXVIII, no. 2 (April 1953), p. 329.

6. ———, "Casework with the Aged: Developments & Trends," Council on Education Seminar, Aspen, Colorado, September 1958, pp. 1–54. Reprinted with permission of the Council on Social Work Education.

7. Ernest W. Burgess, "The Family as a Unity of Interacting Personalities," *The Family* (March 1926).

8. Adaline Buffington, "Francis Bardwell on the Future Care of the Aged," *The Family* (March 1929).

9. Francis Bardwell, "Public Outdoor Relief and the Care of the Aged in Massachusetts," *Social Service Review* (June 1930).

10. Virginia Robinson, *A Changing Psychology in Social Casework* (Chapel Hill: The University of North Carolina Press, 1934).

11. Frances H. McLean, "Exploratory Notes," *The Family* (March 1936).

12. Grace Browning, "Social Service and the Aged," *The Family* XVII, (December 1936).

13. "The Adventure of Old Age," *The Family* (February 1938).

14. William Posner, "Casework with the Aged: Developments & Trends," op. cit., p. 22.

15. Ibid., p. 30.

6   "GO OUT AND BRIGHTEN THE FUTURE"

. . . . . about summing up and looking ahead

THE LAST QUOTATION of the last chapter was from Posner's last article, but the sense of just beginning had been there all along. The years had passed. His involvement had broadened. He had reviewed the history and the growth. He had looked out and back for the sake of his consuming subject, one aged individual, any one in need.

As must be already obvious, as he looked he asked questions and probed within. Depth was always there with the length and the breadth. He wanted to know the reasons why for the programs and the services and for the lack of them. He called for more study so we could know more about theories of development and behavior with old people. He doubted attitudes and explored the values behind them. He evaluated action—what good did it do, what more could we do? All this began with his beginning in the field and was still going on at his ending.

He asked that we be our own severest critics, that with constant and continuing re-evaluation of method and practice we might continue on the road to greater knowledge, greater skill and greater enrichment. And he dared to be that kind of critic himself. Recognizing the increasing awareness of the meaning of socio-cultural factors in human lives, he looked for its influence on casework with the aged. As far as he could see the influence was only superficial. An intellectual understanding was being accepted but it didn't fit his use of the term acceptance—a real integration of ideas that could not help but affect practice.

Agencies as well as caseworkers received their part in the self-appraising criticism. Agencies, institutions, resist change of ways. New knowledge meant new views of social need, but broadening the scope of practice to encompass changing patterns of community and social life meant change. Although change usually met resistance and resistance became a block to progress, on the other hand, when there was a need for change recognized and action instituted, Posner had to question the tendency to change too quickly. Consequently some meaningful traditional services were discarded in unconsidered haste to follow a new fad.

His impatience with the profession was sometimes blunt and condemning, and yet there was compassion and understanding. The use of a quote from Nathan Cohen shows this:

> Two major wars and a major depression forced social work to hasten its pace before it was fully prepared to walk and to articulate concepts before it was ready to talk. There has not been sufficient time and leisure to evaluate the direction it has been taking. There is always the danger, in this type of growth, of becoming so involved in the job to be done that earlier purposes and goals fade into the background. . . . In looking at itself social work must evaluate not only its present but also its heritage from the past and its aspirations for the future.[1]

Posner's evaluations were not only clear and knowledgeable, but had in them a humility that one might wish were not so rare.

> In approaching the subject of non-institutional services for the aged and the challenges implied in them, I am tempted to give voice to a caution which is all too often forgotten by professionals in all fields. We look upon our views as axiomatic and our pronouncements as being all wise and all knowing. We do not realize as often as we should that our attitudes, our thinking, and our feelings

about a subject at any given time may at best be only temporary and ephemeral, changing not only as we gain new knowledge, but changing also as the society in which we live changes, and second, that in the historical process, we often return to old verities, to concepts, attitudes and programs which might have been rejected at an earlier time, but which now at a later date begin to take on new meaning, new form and new content.

Perhaps it is like the pendulum which swings in one direction then to the other and then again to the point from which it started. And perhaps like the pendulum, we too often go to extremes and at any given time various concepts, programs and activities become dominant to the exclusion of others. It is, I suppose, part of human frailty that we are so often unable to see the totality of things or the relationship between past and present, between time and space.[2]

Those things which Posner aimed for and hoped for in the future have become obvious from his estimate of present and past, but while so much depends on altering attitudes, these in turn can be influenced by action. Much that he so zealously supported in early works is taken for granted now; much that he accomplished has already had its affect on the values of both profession and society.

In summing up, he acknowledged that attitudes had been changing and many stereotypes had undergone revision at the same time new concepts on the types of care required by older persons had developed. No longer were all older people considered dependent, in need of protection. No longer was it assumed that aging inevitably means mental deterioration and emotional instability. Less often were the aged grouped together in a category when it came to helping. More often each was seen instead as an individual with his own unique strengths and weaknesses and his own way of responding to particular helping processes—processes that with the aged especially need to be individually chosen, for the more years and experiences are added to a life, the more a unique individuality develops.

And yet, he saw so much still to be done. He knew withdrawal from a problem helps no one. To face it instead, to struggle with it, to make it a focus—that was to him the way. He asked for a willingness to steadfastly work at comprehending the differences and likenesses in helping older people. Only this way he saw as the way of growth.

In various articles, his stocktaking included specific directions. In attempting to synthesize and summarize the challenges he saw, they seem to fall roughly into four areas— new knowledge, modifying practice principles, more social action, and values.

NEW KNOWLEDGE

"The greatest task of all is our own learning. Therein lies the beginning of wisdom."

The first need he found for learning concerned the ways of human development in later years, the influence on that development of early life experiences, and an understanding of stresses and strains, the meanings of problems and capacities, the pains and joys. His questions that have already been mentioned—what does it mean to be lonely and rejected? what is the meaning to older people of time, of separation? what does it mean to them to need help?—concerned with what it is like to be old, indicate the answers he hoped would be found by study and research.

Many of the questions were new to the thought of his time. The meaning of sex to older persons, for instance, was an area that had hardly been touched, perhaps because of our own fears or an embarrassed denial of sexual needs for the old. In the same way, what was the meaning of death as it becomes more imminent, the fears and the reactive symptoms? And what of money, that symbol of self-esteem and prestige and adequacy, what new meaning does it assume when it stops coming in and a life's savings begin to disappear?

Such examples as these put Posner in the role of opening

doors with his line of thought. All have been developed since then, and if answers applicable to practice are only beginning to be used, still they are subjects considered worthy of serious study.

For the increase of knowledge, especially for that dealing with human growth and development in later years, Posner saw a giant gap in our educational system and the immediate future as the time for remedy. No wonder, he felt, that so few social workers became involved with the aged, when the aged were so ignored in development and method classes, when there was so little case material for using, when the possibilities for field work placements with the aged had been barely touched. There was a change in this area during the decade of the '60s, but it is doubtful that Posner would have considered it more than a beginning.

Part of continuing education, too, came within the scope of his concern as he saw the need for a careful and caring supervision of caseworkers, especially to help young workers see aging as a basic part of the life process. They needed, he thought, distinctive help in developing the techniques of working with older people and in sharpening their discernment of the degree of a person's readiness and ability to involve his will and use the help and the helper to the limit of his ability and degree of readiness. They needed, too, distinctive support with their frustrations about societal treatment and shortage of resources. Perhaps, he suggested, caseworkers could be given the stimulation to keep going amid the frustrations by being led to see the creativity needed to work with the aged within the limited resources.

As he named the paths to be taken for learning, his usual wide perception saw the results of learning as gains for everybody. He saw the significance of the questions transcending the immediate interest, of equal moment to all of social work. Many of the specific processes used in casework with the aging may have come from experience in other functional areas but also much of what was being learned about practice in casework with the aging could have great value to casework practice in the other areas of social work as well. He foresaw the enlargement of the horizons of casework with the aging and increasing security in its practice as contributing to the understanding of growth and behavior in all age groups, for he found more to aging than just older years.

MODIFYING PRINCIPLES FOR PRACTICE

All of the factors Posner brought out for special understanding of the aged could be considered working principles for the process of helping. Some of them he picked out as particularly in need of further concentration and development. Just as he had seen the possibility of gain in casework with the aged spreading to other areas, he had often reminded us of the applicability of generic principles to the specific. And always he emphasized the need for modifica‑ tion of generic principles for the aged in general and the need in practice for interpreting the general according to the specific individual older person concerned. He saw this as the only answer to rid our society of stereotyped thinking, with special significance for the aged because it is often difficult to comprehend the balance between inner and outer stresses.

That he believed each individual should have as much *independence* as he could handle is apparent. So is his faith that the older person can assume more responsibility than we allow. He wanted to give the older person a sense of security and responsibility for himself. He wanted to develop a sense of independence in both young and old, so that lives could become emotionally stable and secure without the need for imposing their will on each other. Only through the security of each, he felt, could satisfactory interrelationships be developed.

In one place, he referred to a "principle of choice,"[3] saying that there is no more fundamental principle in casework, and yet so often there are either no choices available for the elderly or we take the easy way of making decisions for them. This says to the older person that we grant him neither the respect nor ability to decide for himself. He felt we need more exploration of the nature of our protectiveness and the use of our authority. Allow choices. Beware of overprotection. And yet be prepared for the times when the agency has to assume a total responsibility. When dependence is clearly necessary, further understanding of its implications is needed. What does it mean to the person in the dependent position, and how do we best work with it?

Closely allied with strengthening the sense of self in the individual through granting a measure of independence and responsibility, was his concern with the *roles* they are allowed, or rather not allowed. He felt that so much of what we do is aimed at doing *for* older people, with not enough thinking and planning to establish the kinds of programs in which they themselves can actively participate. He saw community programs such as serving as volunteers in hospitals, and as friendly visitors to both young and old as a beginning step, but hoped for much more as he recalled the experience during World War II when people retired or ready for retirement were employed in essential war production jobs. The transformation of those who became truly useful again was a phenomenon he would like us to recall and act upon.

Now and even more in the future of earlier retirements, he felt we must use our best thinking in finding new roles for older people, new ways of utilizing their wisdom, maturity and experience. The importance of role for every person is taken for granted now. The concept was new at the time he wrote:

> We want an acceptance by individuals of the changing pace of living so that they can find expression in different roles. This requires a flexibility in our attitudes and in our mores. The loss of certain functions does not mean the loss of self, but means the acceptance of other functions—new ones—which are pertinent to age and status. We want an educational process in living that will help the individual to accept the changing roles in living so

that each stage is accepted with greater ease and with satisfaction.[4]

He only touched on this, the need for a pursuit of thought stressing the concept of aging as a phenomenon in all of living. With more awareness aging would be seen as something not only for the old but for all as we grow from one phase of life, one set of roles, into another phase with new roles.

One of the roles he saw as important was that of being a part of a family. It is both an outgrowth of the need for role and a part of the principle of wholeness:

> We need to feel that the older person or persons are "families" in their own right. They do not stop being such by virtue of age or because children have left the household. The family is a continuity, whether there are five people in it or just one person. It is only as each has this feeling of individual wholeness that there can be togetherness and interrelatedness.[5]

Much as he had said about *generational component* and *socio-cultural* influences, he felt they were still concepts that were yet to come fully alive in practice.

> The crucial question is: How far have we really rooted our practice generationally? Have we translated theory into practice? Are we as adept in making socio-cultural diagnoses as we are in making psycho-social diagnoses? Do we really understand generational patterns of behavior? Do we really understand the socio-cultural basis for our own actions, biases, prejudices? What have agencies done to make themselves available with real understanding to diverse cultural groups and what have they done to make cultural knowledge available to casework practitioners?[6]

For generational peace, within families and communities, he wanted to see settings where the roles of the younger and older members are more clearly defined and accepted in terms of their interrelationship with each other. To give the older person status without isolating him was just another seed idea planted by Posner.

To do this, to integrate persons of different generations and still maintain the status of each, he saw room for new developments in *communication,* mainly centering his attention around communication between workers and older clients in order to go on and improve communication within the families and communities. He wanted our processes to by dynamic and creative ones and saw communication as the very tool to work with in all phases of our work. By sharpening this tool he felt it would be possible for us to go beyond the individual relationship and develop new services to help the aging person to grow and live.

Although it comes under the cover of individualizing, in finding new ways for according status to the older person, Posner saw such a need for more emphasis on *flexibility* of the casework process that he put it in a separate category in his view of future directions. He felt that much of the good achieved by his own agency had come through a flexibility of approach with easy access allowed from one service as needed to the other as needed. He called it a theory of progression and individual need. There was a need for flexibility in the old principle of permanence:

> When we think of care for the aged we are usually inclined to think of the need for a permanent plan. This has been basic to institutional philosophy and has been a factor retarding the development of non-institutional services. Certainly our experience in providing services for the aged has not borne this out. Although it is true that many older persons need long-time care, it does not mean permanent care. The individualization of older persons has also helped us to see their differential needs; with continued community living as the major goal of all of our services we have seen our services as being rehabilitative in nature. This ties in, too, with the principle of progression . . . namely that the type of service offered has to be geared to the degree of the older person's handi-

cap, with a need to shift services back and forth based upon client need.[7]

So a principle of non-permanence or flexibility evolves, one that includes the partialization of casework process— the step by step solution to problems rather than the drastic approach. It is a principle that he saw holding true whether around an appointment time that has to be changed, or a home visit that has to be made instead of an office visit, in an adjustment of the planned length of service or in helping the hard-to-reach person participate in the helping relationship.

To help that hard-to-reach person there is the need to be flexible, too, about another principle sometimes held dear in other areas; that is, that in order to use help one must take it upon himself to reach for that help. With the elderly there has to be a place for *outreach*. We must be able to go out to those who have no way of knowing of the service, or once knowing, are fearful of approach. And even once touched, we have to do more to maintain the contact and sustain the motivation.

It would seem to me that there has to be . . . a greater concern for those older persons in the community who never reach the agency doors but who still need help, a greater concern for those living in settings which do not provide the benefits that may be available in the family agency. As agencies and as individuals we must reach out to these older persons and to these settings. For too long a time the helping professions, social work among them, have sat back and waited for the community to come to them. The time has come, I believe, to recapture some of the zeal and initiative that characterized our ways of working in earlier days. Therein lies the challenge for our days, too.[8]

MORE SOCIAL ACTION

"We are not only social workers; we are citizens, too. This means that as we sharpen our knowledge and skills as social workers, we must also be active in modifying the thinking of society as a whole."[9]

We broaden and deepen our knowledge and understanding. We deepen and strengthen our particular principles and skills. We share with society our goals. We work with society toward those goals. As a caseworker and a man of social action, Posner kept the evolving goals in sight. In 1957, some were:

> With respect to living arrangements, we want a new emphasis on the value of community living arrangements for the older person, and on the privacy and independence that comes with it. We want the development of facilities that will give the older person security in his privacy and eliminate much of the fear that is now felt by many—fears of illness and isolation. We want a variety of facilities which will respond to the *individual* needs of the older person.

Progress has been made. Enough?

> We want a variety of housing projects for those who can care for themselves, so designed as to conserve as much energy as possible and to prevent accidents. These projects need not be exclusively for the aged; we need the intermingling of generations. We would want to provide for guidance and helping facilities which would encourage the older person to seek companionship and participate in activities in other communities and groups.

Progress has been made. Enough?

> We want congregate forms of care, such as homes for the aged and hospitals for the chronically ill, only for those who need that type of care, but not for the well or ambulatory aged who should be encouraged to live in community settings and to benefit from them. And in homes for aged and in hospitals for chronically ill, we want rehabilitation programs that will look to the dis-

charge of older persons to other community settings, so that the congregate facilities become *means to ends* and not *ends* in themselves.[10]

Progress has been made. Enough?

To get, or begin to get, these and all the other desirable changes—in employment, medical care, recreation, etc.— Posner saw the interrelationship of one to another. As he prepared for the White House Conference in 1961, he concluded that the time was past when those interested in housing or medical care or social service were interested only in their own subject. Now concern was broad and all inclusive. There was a realization that a partial approach to aging could not bring adequate answers. There was a realization of the need not for isolated activity but for interdisciplinary activity.

The interdisciplinary approach was not new. It just needed expansion. He hoped for more acceptance in casework with the aged of the need to call upon the physician, the psychiatrist, the public health nurse, the employment agency, the welfare agency, the minister and all others concerned. It was an approach that would help break down our exclusiveness. At the same time he had no doubt that it would also help to clarify the real and distinct contribution of the social worker.

Considering the relationships of agencies and agencies, of agencies and community, he drew attention first to the nature of the relationship among professional staffs of the agencies:

> I firmly believe this to be basic if social need is to be met. Without overburdening the term, may I say that it is the security of the agency administration and staff which determines the degree of interagency cooperation. Given this security, walls can literally tumble to make way for the meeting of social need. When this exists we become less concerned with auspices of programs; we have less need to be rigid about our way; we become

more attuned to interdisciplinary approaches. In our community it was this kind of relationship that made it possible for us to develop a foster home program for mental patients with a voluntary mental hospital, and to provide homemakers to another agency without the fear that we would be swallowed up. It is this same security which made it possible for us to accept some "control" by the public agencies in return for grants of money to meet social need, without the fear of having to give up our philosophy and essential function. On the other hand, in a community not far from here, they have not been able to establish cooperative programs because the family agency people and hospital people do not talk to each other. It is this *inner factor* which to me seems basic to meeting social need. There are risks, to be sure, but these are the kinds of risks that as social workers we must learn to take.[11]

Within the agency, Posner continued to see a specialized structure as a source of growth. What he had in mind at the time he wrote, has become better known as the principle of concentration. He emphasized that they had given themselves the luxury of concentration as a way to development. And yet he did not want to glorify specialization for its own sake. In their experiences it had simply become an effective means to a desired end—the development of special knowledge and skills and out of this more and better services. He was not ruling out other means. He was only emphasizing the success of theirs, and seemed to feel a time of concentration could lead to a return to a more complete integration of the aged in general services without the old neglect.

Getting to the specific programs that he saw as needed or needing expansion, Posner sought the development of social and community programs that would offer opportunities for the participation of all age groups so that each one's role could be seen more clearly and thus be more acceptable. There had been little, if any, such inclusive action but he found the day centers for the aged of value in the meantime, giving participants new interest, new companionship, perhaps a new lease on life. He gave credit to Departments of Welfare offering supplementary services such as recreation centers, medical and other services. He commended the clubs and the camps, the geriatric clinics and rehabilitation centers, the hospital home care programs, the sheltered workshops. He commended and asked for more.

One of the specific services that he favored and saw as one of tremendous potential given professional social work study and training and continuing guidance, was that of friendly visiting. He was thinking of the many aged who can manage fairly well on their own but who are socially isolated and almost always alone. They urgently need the establishment of human contact and the feeling of still being counted as human beings. To such a shut-in, the friendly visitor represents a person who brings the outside world in, a friend to talk to, a someone who cares. Again Posner remembered the reciprocity of the benefit gained.

The service could be used, too, as a tool for the reaching out. He described his agency's experimental program of going into a rooming house area known to be populated by many older persons. Supplied with names given to them by community people, the friendly visitors went out to visit. Some of the older people at first rejected the overtures of a visit, but the friendly visitors continued to go back. Most were eventually admitted. The potential of this kind of contact for the prevention of deterioration was substantiated.

Posner saw prevention by preparation, by education, as an essential part of society's thinking about the future of its citizens. Without it, the scope of servicing the growing numbers of aged with the limited services offered would be intolerable. He thought education about aging would help for persons of all ages and ways and means of preparing people for aging should be developed. As children are prepared for school, students for careers, and young people for marriage, so people of younger years need preparation for the changing circumstances of older years.

VALUES

Getting full circle back to where we began, the future continues to call for practical action that will have an influence on slowing or halting the deterioration of aging, and for a concomitant change of attitudes and examination of the values behind them. To Posner, our value systems needed constant reexamination. He felt we had not yet thought through or integrated properly the values that shape our lives and bear upon our professional knowledge and techniques. He did not see it as something to be done lightly or painlessly, but as a continuing responsibility accomplished only by clear and ruthlessly honest self-evaluation of our individual selves and of our profession.

He suggested that as social work developed as a profession, perhaps in its desire to gain status, it had allowed its values system to approve some needs and ways of meeting needs as more highly professional than others. For instance, once giving financial assistance was a major function of family agencies and meeting the need ranked high. Important as it was, its ranking went down as the knowledge and skill and status of counseling went up.

Applied to the aging, he termed "the inner factor" as basic to what might be accomplished. For it is the inner factor within each that must be free to develop a conviction about the value of giving service to the aged, a conviction which may come only after considerable struggle. Then service for the aged can become part of the value system of ourselves and our agencies and we can carry that conviction and those values to other agencies and to the community.

Finally:

In all that has been said, we want for the future the development of secure people, no matter what their age; people who will *continue to strive* and for whom added years mean maturity, and whose philosophy of life will be expressed in terms of what they themselves have yet to live for, in terms of growth and change.

All, then, that is asked is a reaffirmation of our faith in the dignity of men. In this pioneering field we can still lead the way to a renewed emphasis upon the growth potentialities of all persons regardless of age or condition. But that can hardly be done unless our "belief in people" includes the conviction that the aged are people too.[12]

Notes

1. Nathan E. Cohen, *Social Work in the American Tradition* (New York, The Dryden Press, 1958).

2. William Posner, "A Case History of the Development of Non-Institutional Services for the Aged," Florida Council on Aging, May 1958, p. 1.

3. ———, "New Horizons in Casework with the Aged, "Welfare and Health Council of New York City, March 1955, p. 13.

4. ———, "Adapting and Sharpening Social Work Knowledge and Skills in Serving the Aged," *Social Work* 2, no. 4 (October 1957), p. 41.

5. Ibid.

6. ———, "Characteristics of Casework with Older People—A Discussion of Basic Issues," National Committee on Aging, October 1960, p. 18.

7. ———, "A Case History of the Development of Non-Institutional Services for the Aged," op. cit., pp. 5–7.

8. Ibid., p. 8.

9. ———, "Adapting and Sharpening Social Work Knowledge and Skills in Serving the Aged," op. cit., p. 41.

10. Ibid., p. 42.

11. William Posner, "The Effect of Changing Social Need on Interagency and Community Relations," *Journal of Social Work Process* XI, (1960), p. 56.

12. ———, "Adapting and Sharpening Social Work Knowledge and Skills in Serving the Aged," op. cit., p. 42.

"LET ANYONE WHO IS HUNGRY COME AND EAT"

..... about Jewishness

WILLIAM POSNER WAS a Jew and embraced all that meant in faith and tradition and culture. At the same time he neither imposed his own response to being a Jew upon others nor judged anyone whose beliefs and ways were different than his own. However, as a Jewish social worker in a Jewish agency serving Jewish clients through the largess of a Jewish community, he found the Jewish factor in social work one that could not be put aside as irrelevant. Whatever meaning being a Jew or not being a Jew might have to a worker, whatever meaning being a Jew might have or not have to a client, the Jewishness remained a fact to be faced. Posner strongly supported the facing of any facts in all of social work practice.

For him a Jewish social agency was an instrument of the Jewish community. No matter what its function might be, an agency would represent the Jewish community to the client. Some clients came to Jewish agencies for lack of similar services elsewhere. Some clients chose a Jewish agency precisely because it was Jewish. For all clients, in whatever group they fall, the agency's Jewishness had some special meaning. In writing of their experience, Posner and Saul Hofstein[1] claimed it important to look for this special meaning at the time of the first contact. Either an expression of feelings on the subject or the absence of an expression of feelings could be of real psychological significance in the work ahead. In some cases, people may just feel more at ease with someone they feel is their own kind in stating a problem directly and accepting help. It may be the one thing the client can see he has in common with worker or agency.

For instance, there was the client who expected that because he came to a Jewish agency his every need or desire would be met regardless of whether or not the agency was set up for the purpose, or whether or not it felt the client could really be helped with the service. In such cases the Jewishness of the agency could constitute a problem in helping the client face realistically the limited conditions under which the agency could provide help.

On the other hand there were other clients who were fearful of the particular Jewish ideology the agency represented, or the demands or expectations the agency might make upon them. As one client put it, he hoped they would not suggest prayer as the solution to his problem. Such an attitude on the part of the client could be related to a fear around coming to the agency for help. The Jewishness of the agency could intensify such fear. Whatever meaning the Jewishness of the agency had for the client, they felt it was essential that the worker be prepared to deal with it.

Throughout their history as a dispersed people, the Jews have sought for and centered on meaning in life. Social work, too, looks for meanings. That Jewish people have become leaders in progressive social work is apparent. Posner was one of those leaders, especially for the old, and especially in promoting the acceptance and use of Jewishness in social work with the old. As a part of his case for its continuation he studied and presented the history of Jewish social work. He went back to its beginnings in the synagogue where social service was taken for granted as being as important as religion and education.

After the early nineteenth century, mutual aid societies developed unrelated to the synagogue, and as the Jewish population increased, more varied institutions were established such as hospitals, charity agencies, orphan asylums, homes for the aged. He found the increase in the Jewish population was only one of the reasons for such institutions. The basic motive was a religio-cultural one. A fear of proselytism led to the development of Jewish child care agencies. A need for kosher food had a part in the establishment of Jewish hospitals and other institutions.

During the years of development there was a good deal of conflict within and between the Jewish social agencies and the Jewish community on whether or not there need be such a thing as "Jewish content" in their social work. It was usually handled according to the way any particular worker felt about it. Most often it was considered a fallacious notion that there was anything to distinguish Jewish social work from any other social work, until around the mid-20th century.

Suffice it to say that the causes of the renewed interest in Jewishness must be sought for both in the contemporary history of American Jewry and in the developments in casework theory and practice. . . . The primary concern of the largest segment of American Jewry until relatively recently was assimilation into the American scene. The effect of this assimilative trend upon the Jewish social agency was to change its emphasis from a religio-cultural orientation to one that was predominantly secular. Concurrently, casework theory was shifting its concern from an emphasis upon external and environmental factors to one which brought into focus the internal structure of personality. These two trends operating simultaneously upon the Jewish social agency tended to lead to the subordination of Jewishness to a secondary position.

Currently both of the trends cited above have been shifting again in the other direction. With so large a proportion of the Jewish population today reared and educated in American institutions, assimilation as such is no longer as vital an issue as it was a generation ago. Rather there is a growing concern within the new generation reared away from Jewish culture, somehow to integrate into its experience more of the cultural background which would bring it closer to its heritage. The [World War II] holocaust, its particular effect upon the Jewish people, and the rebirth of Israel have also stimulated an intense and widespread interest in Jewish contemporary culture and communal life. In casework, too, with the firm establishment of the importance of psychological dynamics and personal relationship, there is a renewed interest in both the role played by cultural factors in personality formation and the use of an understanding of those factors in casework and counseling. As the earlier trends cited had resulted in the subordination of Jewishness in Jewish social agencies, so these present trends are having the reverse effect of reawakening interest in Jewishness on the part of Jewish social workers.[2]

Granted, then, that Jewishness is a fact of life for a Jewish client or a Jewish worker or a Jewish agency. It may or may not be relevant to helping in all cases but cannot be simply overlooked. Often the response of social work would have to be primarily focused on the meaning of that particular fact of life to that particular person. It is a reality that may be used as a tool in helping—or may not.

In their article Posner and Hofstein said that after their first conclusion on the importance of being aware of the status of Jewishness with a client in casework, they began to find variations in the way the Jewish factor affected a case. In some situations the core problem might concern an internal conflict of a client about his own Jewishness. Or there might be a problem in relationship caused by differences in Jewish orientation between the persons involved.

For instance, a client had changed his name and tried to separate himself completely from his Jewishness but only at the expense of considerable guilt and anxiety. In another case a parent had come to the agency with the complaint that his daughter was associating with non-Jewish boys. In many cases of marital counseling, the conflict grew from a mixed marriage. Knowing that many psychological dynamics enter into such situations, the importance of Jewishness as a factor was increasingly recognized. No wonder that Posner stressed the need of the caseworker to have an understanding of the cultural backgrounds within which and sometimes because of which problems grew.

Combining his review of the history of Jewish social work with his knowledge of the development of social work in general, he found the change in the American family of special importance. The Jewish people were mainly recent immigrants who had experienced great change. They were essentially first or second generation families, the adults or their parents having immigrated to this country. Such transfer from one society to another, with its separation from the old, naturally led to feelings of insecurity and isolation, and with some to a desire to submerge themselves in the dominant group around them.

The Jewish group's contact with the new world had within it the seeds of both adjustment and alienation. On the one hand, economic necessity and the need to find employment in the community forced a measure of integration and adjustment. On the other hand, the tendency in a strange land to live among one's own, to go to one's former countrymen for assistance, to set up religious and cultural institutions according to the way it was done in the old country, made for alienation from the new environment. All of these pressures in addition to his loneliness and lack of sense of belonging created many contradictions in the Jewish immigrant's behavior.

If it has not already been apparent, at this point mention must be made of the validity of the Posner thoughts on ethnic identity and their application by helping professions in the later times around the problems of Negroes, Mexicans, and Indians. What he said of the Jewish experience fits other groups, whether ethnic, economic, aged, handicapped or whatever the likeness might be. His answer, affirmation of difference, was repeatedly stressed years before "black is beautiful."

To go on with the contradictions in the minority's behavior, he quotes from Bernard Weinryb:

> "Hopelessness and a sense of wanting to achieve; resistance to change and willingness to give up old ways and mores; clinging to group identity, yet having the urge for assimilation; religious piety and laxity; political conservatism and radicalism."[3]

> *One of the characteristics of an insecure minority is to try to accept the behavior patterns, the fashions and values of the majority group and by the same token also accept or internalize the low esteem the majority has for them.*

(Italics mine to again draw attention to the applicability of his understanding of Jewishness to other "lesser" peoples.)

> The individual begins to accept as valid the stereotypes attributed to him by the majority culture. As a result many Jews during the early part of the century developed a sense of self-hatred which also transmitted itself to family and children in the form of a denial of their socio-cultural heritage. However, as new opportunities opened for him, the immigrant worker rose economically. The Jew, having come from an urban culture, manifested a high degree of occupational and class mobility. He and his children gradually became part of the urbanized, industrialized American middle class. He became as much part of our "other-directed" and market society as did his middle class Protestant neighbor. Contrarily, his emergence and accommodation to his American environment had lessened the need for assimilation, self-denial and self-hatred. The result was a return to his socio-cultural heritage. In our day, as the desire for group identification increases, we are beginning to see the emergence of a Jewish group which has accommodated itself socio-economically, in language, in external way of life to the American environment and culture, but which clings to its heritage, activates Jewish values, and has an emotional attachment to the Jewish group.[4]

With the older Jewish people described, the continuity of their cultural heritage provides a stability to be clung to and to .be preserved for future generations. It is to them the temporarily alienated young must return to find their ethnic identity. In so doing can the young give to the old a purpose for being.

Concluding their article, Posner and Hofstein emphasized that it was not their contention that the basic casework and counseling process was different in a Jewish agency than in any other type of agency. They saw no basic differences between Jew and non-Jew in personality structure or in the dynamics of relationship. There was no Jewish casework process. They did believe, however, that each person tends to find expression for his personality and internal needs in the culture of which he is a part.

Along with the cultural inheritance and the fact of being one of a distinct people, there is for many, of course, the religious part of being Jewish. How does this affect the family, the client, the agency, the worker? Is it something that means nothing or everything, and as always with social work, how do we use whatever response the individual makes as an aid toward fulfillment? As with culture, the religious status of the client must be considered.

Posner saw that regardless of his point of origin, the Jew brought with him to this country the attitudes, traditions, customs and practices he lived by in the old country. These aspects of living, transmitted to him by his forebears, were rooted in biblical tradition. This was as true for family relationships as it was of specific religious practices. The respective roles of the father, mother, children, grandparents, and the interrelationships between them were determined by biblical authority. From the Bible in practice attitudes toward older family members were clearly positive. So were the customs and facilities developed for their care in the community.

The individual clients will have as varied a religious dedication as there are clients. For some the agency represents the "conscience" of the Jewish community. For these clients bringing a problem to the Jewish agency implies that they are disclosing it to the Jewish community which it represents. Such an action might arouse a fear of leaving themselves open to condemnation. For other clients the fact that the Jewish agency is ready to accept their problem and help them with it may have the symbolical significance of forgiveness. If the Jewish social agency does not need to condemn them, then maybe their own condemnation of themselves need not be so great. Other clients in other agencies may know a similar relief on first experiencing the nonjudgmental social work principle of acceptance in action, but for the Jew of faith there can be an added religious element.

How the client lives his religion also becomes a vital factor in resident placement, making it possible for the religious older person to continue his own way of religious practices or nonpractices. In agency procedure, Posner emphasized that there must always be a respect for the client's choice of retaining his own type of Jewishness in any degree of tradition he prefers.

Much of this has been applicable to a Jewish person of any age. For those older people who find importance in religion, it seemed Posner's own convictions came through most clearly in his last article on the White House Conference. Writing in a Jewish magazine, he considered the Conference in its policy statement on Religion and Aging as a highlight. He quoted generously:

> Religion's concern with human dignity at every stage in the span of life derives from the fact that each individual is created in the image of God. As a consequence, religion seeks to build a living fellowship of believers in which the aging find and share the true benefits of being a part of the household of God. . . . Within the life of the congregation each older person should be treated as an individual. Each is entitled to responsible membership within the religious fellowship. Any attitude on the part

of the congregation which hinders the exercise of this right must be regarded as a contradiction of religious teaching. It should rather be its concern to foster relationships calculated to imbue in the elderly a sense of belonging, of being needed and useful in a vital way. This will go far to promote a richer religious experience for the aging and will likewise provide a salutary example to be followed in the family circle and in the outer rings of society.

We underline the obligation of religious groups to instill as an essential of sound family life an attitude of respect for the individuality and intrinsic importance of each aging member. Thus, while both the family and the congregation will feel direct responsibility to provide special services, educational materials, and programs for the aging, every effort should be made to see that these do not involve an unnecessary separation from the main stream of familiar or congregational life. . . . Religion can assist the aging in finding within themselves and in the fellowship of faith the resources to meet those problems and fears which seem inevitably to accompany one's latter years. In illness, trouble, and infirmity as well as in hours of joy and exultation the community of faith offers strength, comfort and benediction in many forms. Religion binds a man to creation and the Creator, and enables him to face the future with hope.[5]

Although he went on to pick up from there some specific things he felt synagogues could do in making older years meaningful years, almost always Posner brought in the Jewish and the religious only as they might influence caring, understanding, and accepting social work. Only in the agency manual on Passover assistance is there a tone other than objective. After briefly explaining the origin of Passover, the history of the tradition in Jewish life, and the specific reasons for the poor to need help at this time in order to celebrate properly, he continues:

Actually, the giving of charity was always an important part of Jewish living. Passover assistance, however, had a special meaning which transcended the bounds of ordinary giving, the roots of which are found in the significance the holiday has taken on through Jewish history.

The holiday signified freedom. It was not merely an ancient freedom which was celebrated but the Jew interpreted the holiday as a hope for continued freedom in those days of enslavement in modern times, and this hope was always combined with a feeling of compassion for those less fortunate. This is expressed simply in the HAGGADAH, the Passover narrative, which was written probably in the third century of the Common era. The very first paragraph of this narrative probably embodies more than others the meaning of the holiday.

> "This is the bread of affliction that our forefathers ate in the land of Egypt. Let anyone who is hungry come and eat. Let anyone who is in want come and celebrate the Passover. . . . This year we are slaves. Next year may we be free men. . . ."[6]

The giving of charity was more than the result of the feeling of a persecuted people for others less fortunate. It was in Judaism a duty commanded by God and supported by Talmud tradition. Posner didn't write of this separately and specifically. He lived it. As a social worker and as a Jew, he lived it.

Judaism, founded on love of God and love of neighbor for God, sees all creation and creatures as precious and believes in the sanctity of life. Inevitably the dignity of the human individual and his right to be himself follow, fundamental social work values. It is here and in acts of charity that the Jews fulfill God's will. Thus their thrust toward benevolence is on the one hand a way of reaching toward unity with God, and on the other a highly religious act in reconciling other men to God.

Several years after his death the National Association of

Jewish Family, Children's and Health Services started an annual "William Posner Memorial Institute" as they felt he so significantly symbolized the contribution of Jewish social work. In the first such institute David Zeff and Irving Greenberg developed ideas of the Jewish tradition of charity, distinguishing between two types or stages. The first is *Zedakah,* the human obligation, the fulfillment of one's duty toward the poor. *Chesed* is more a loving kindness, having a sense of compassion and human kinship, the doing of love to rich as well as poor, transcending the acts of obligation. "The Torah . . . begins and ends with loving kindness as a divine act."[7]

This seems to describe the impetus of the man Posner where Jewishness and social work met in his own life. Zeff and Greenberg go on to say that *Zedakah* (charity) along with *Tfila* and *Torah* (prayer and learning) are the three basic pillars of Judaism, each with the same level of importance. Whereas with most people one part is given priority, from all that those who knew him say about him, it would seem the three were blended in like proportions in the life of William Posner.

Always wanting to learn more in order to give more valuable help, he sought after new knowledge, deeper truths, with the support of daily prayer practices of Orthodox Jewry. Yet some say that few of his professional associates were aware of his adherence to Jewish Orthodoxy. A friend writes that he was one of those rare human beings whose religious beliefs and practices were never made to stand out. He had the great ability to organize his daily life activities so that what he had to do for his religion and his God did not collide with what he had to do for his clients and colleagues.

The "In Memoriam" booklet put out by his synagogue at the time of his death is filled with references to the many things he did in synagogue worship and work. In fact, it seems there was no function that he did not at some time do, preferably without notice or credit. At the same time he was making a deep impression on fellow Jews in the social work field, showing them how secular work could be enriched by the principles of the sacred. Maurice Hexter was the leader for many years of the New York City Federation of Jewish Philanthropies. He wrote:

> William Posner was one of those rare people who truly represented the noblest ideals of Jewish social work. He based his orientation as a social worker on a profound faith in God and a deep concern for the continuity of Judaism. His belief, rather than shutting him off from secular life, became the core of his work, impelling him to seek always more and better ways of serving his fellow man. It was a search that had begun with his earliest efforts as a professional and that he never ceased to pursue.[8]

Again from the comments of friends, they saw his profession and his religion deeply intertwined. Friend Irving Greenberg, now Executive Director of the Jewish Counseling & Service Agency in Newark, discussed in a letter his feeling that Posner saw Jewish social work as related to the continuity of Judaism:

> While we never discussed it, because that was a period in which being Jewish and supporting Judaism made all of us feel self-conscious, I am sure that he would have expressed the Judaic belief that "the poor" were special wards of God. He lived and performed as if he were convinced that the primary responsibility towards the "poor" was the constant search and discovery of what God wanted us to do in their behalf. Therefore, it never really surprised me to see him go into a no man's land, dealing with the foster home care for the elderly. . . .
> His faith and work were inseparable.

These comments were written in response to a specific query about what seemed to me to be a "wholeness" of William Posner's life and work and faith, a unity in all of his being.

Notes

1. William Posner and Saul Hofstein, "The Use of the Agency's Jewishness in Casework Process," *Social Service Quarterly* XXVI (March 1950), pp. 332–40.

2. Ibid.

3. Bernard Weinryb, "Jewish Immigration & Accommodation to America," *American Jewish Historical Society* XLVI (March 1957).

4. William Posner, "Socio-Cultural Factors in Casework with Adult Children and Aged Parents," *Journal of Jewish Communal Service* XXXV, no. 2 (Winter 1958), pp. 195–96.

5. Policy Statement, Religion & Aging Section, White House Conference on Aging, January 1961, in "Aging with a Future," *Jewish Life* (April 1961), pp. 24–25.

6. William Posner, "Manual of Policies and Procedures for Passover Assistance Program," Jewish Community Services of Long Island, March 1952, p. 1.

7. David Zeff and Irving Greenberg, "The Jewish Casework Agency: Problems and Prospects in a Time of Paradox," in *William Posner Memorial Institute,* National Conference of Jewish Communal Service, 1966, pp. 17–18.

8. Maurice Hexter, "A Professional's Professional," in *William Posner: Memorial Journal* (New York: Young Israel of Windsor Park, 1963).

IN ONE WAY OR ANOTHER, Posner spoke of the wholeness of persons and of people united in community throughout his work. It was not set forth in any one section for espousal. It comes through in bits and pieces, in the little here, the little there that made up the whole of his work.

Returning to our focus on working with the person full of years, Posner seemed to literally long for others to share his understanding of old age as a normal and necessary part of the full life and development of a human being, as one phase of the many we pass through, gaining from each its enrichment. When, in his first article from Long Island, he found the dynamics of the casework process helping both older persons and workers towards a philosophy of living rather than one of death, he was finding in the winding up time of life something of its whole essence.

In describing the private residence program, he saw its greatest benefit in the renewal of a sense of self in the older person, a new awareness of continuing capacity for growth. And he saw social work's part to play in developing the most for this last stage, especially in drawing upon that person's own inner resources, those strengths accumulated throughout the years of so much and such varied experience. Then, having been helped to build for himself a new role of *being* for the new age, with a firmly established "individual wholeness," the one of old age can again be interrelated with others in a new way fitted to the new role.

Posner saw those "others" as all members of the community, especially the total family unit, and yet not only that. The distinctive role of simply being an older person could not be distinguished and accepted in isolation from other ages. This, then, was a part of his support of communities integrating all ages into participation together in housing, work, recreation, church and synagogue; in short, in living. In order to maintain older people within the whole of community living, Posner faced the fact that there could rarely be a totality in one service. To be of real help to any person, but especially to the old, to be of service to the whole person, he knew there might be a need for several services at one time or for many services at different times. In fact, a worker with the old might be taking on the awesome responsibility for a person's whole range of needs, whole life.

To educate and train and inspire workers toward the need of a more complete giving of self in service to the aged, Posner held fast to his conviction about the necessity for separated concentration of effort. Perhaps because he believed so strongly in integration in other areas, because he opposed fragmentation of work and people, he had to support specialization so firmly. Granting that generic casework principles apply with modification to the old, hoping that agencies could achieve a high standard of service to the aged without having to separate services, he did not see at the time of his writing that this was possible considering current attitudes. He therefore continued to favor segmentation only to provide the opportunity for concentration that would lead eventually to the separated part becoming more truly a part of the whole.

And he knew that social work itself was only a part. So he sought more working together in unity of purpose among agencies, among professions, among community resources, all integrating efforts toward complete services to maintain and provide that wholeness of the older person.

Finally, considering any one life in its entirety of years, he wanted a new orientation to "aging" as a concept so that it would become a part of our helping of younger people too. Here aging would be recognized as applying to all ages. We grow up and mature, we give up some things and take on others as we go from each age and stage to the next. His concern was not only for the old but for the young. His concern was not only for the present but for the future as well. To develop and inculcate positive attitudes toward aging in younger generations would help to prevent some of the deteriorating aspects of aging that come from psychological separation.

So William Posner had a conviction about the wholeness of life and the oneness of the human race. Looking back at his work, it seems a testimony to that faith. His basic theme was to keep the old counting among the living, to keep the aged years a part of all of life. Can his influence be measured? His thought was a part of his work and his time and his culture. Much of it was neither new nor unique—only expressed in different ways and places. Some of it was both new and unique—the ideas on generations and ethnic identities and caseworker culture, for instance— and yet they were concepts that were probably rising concomitantly in other minds and other locations. The influence that cannot be put on a list or measured on a scale was the crusading drive to bring down from the shelf neglected human beings and restore them to a rightful and respected place among people.

As a part of Posner's own wholeness of being, apparently his own life and his own convictions could not be separated. They were one. Going through the words written about him by those who knew him, phrases stand out to strengthen this, my conviction, about him. "A man so simple" he was called, and one who did so much could not be so termed unless all that he did was simply a part of one integrated life. He didn't just speak, he acted, they say. He didn't have a modest air, he was the embodiment of modesty. He didn't preach, he practiced. He didn't give charity, he lived it.

　　To William Posner these afflicted human beings were all "bekirbcho" in his midst; were all *his* problems and objects of *his* training and love.[1]

(Again the italics are mine, for they tell me "bekirbcho" means "within him.")

It has been said his religion and profession were deeply intertwined, that if he had been able to go on to teach as planned at the Wurzweiler School of Social Work, he would have been able to convey the deep relationship between the spiritual and rational in social work. It seems to me that in William Posner, the professional and religious, the spiritual and rational, the secular and sacred, were not merely intertwined, they were blended into the singleness of being that is true integrity.

When death comes before the three score and ten years, it is so often termed "untimely," a time before life on earth has reached completion. The term was used about Posner, who died at age 48. Yet he believed in the later years as intended for a rounding out and a tying up of all a person's life, a period of fulfillment. Perhaps his death, then, was not really so untimely. Perhaps his life had early attained a fruition unrelated to years.

Note

1. Fabian Schonfeld, "A Servant of Humanity," in *William Posner Memorial Journal* (New York: Young Israel of Windsor Park, 1963).

APPENDIX A

William Posner's Life

1913—Born, Brooklyn, New York
1933—B.S.S. City College of New York
1937—M.S.W. University of Pennsylvania, School of Social Work
1937–1939—Caseworker, Association for Jewish Children of Philadelphia
1939–1948—District Supervisor, Jewish Child Care Association of New York
1948–1960—Assistant Director, Jewish Community Services of Long Island: also Supervisor of Services for the Aged
1960–1961—Executive Director, Jewish Community Services of Long Island
1961 (April 16)—Deceased

Memberships

National Association of Social Workers
National Conference on Social Welfare
National Conference of Jewish Communal Services
New York State Welfare Conference
Fellow, Gerontological Society
National Committee on the Aging
Chairman, Division of the Aged, Community Council of Greater New York
Chairman, Division on the Aged, Queensboro Council for Social Welfare

143

Chairman, Division on the Aged, Health and Welfare Council of Nassau County

Book Review Editor, *Journal of Jewish Communal Service*

Treasurer, National Conference of Jewish Communal Service

Author of 52 or more scholarly papers on Child Care, Family Services, and the Aged

AWARDS

Mr. Posner was honored by the Council on Jewish Federations and Welfare Funds in 1956 with the William Schroder Award for agency work with the aged.

In 1959, he received the first "Outstanding Jewish Social Worker" Award from the Commission on Synagogue Relations of the Federation of Jewish Philanthropies of New York.

Mr. Posner was recognized nationally as an authority on social services for the aged and served as a consultant to the White House Conference. He was appointed by Governor Rockefeller as an official delegate to the White House Conference on Aging from New York State.

He served as a lecturer at the New York School of Psychiatry, New York State Department of Mental Hygiene, and at the Yeshiva University School of Social Work.

Mr. Posner was appointed Associate Professor at the Yeshiva University School of Social Work and had planned to join the faculty in September, 1961.

APPENDIX B

FAMILY AIDE SERVICE

(from the Manual of Policies and Procedures in the
Division on Services for the Aged
of the Jewish Community Services of Long Island)

The most typical situations in which Family Aide service would be given are the following:

1. A temporary acute, non-contagious illness of the elderly person.

2. A temporary emergency in the situation of an adult child who cares for an aged parent.

3. For a definite interim waiting period for admission to an institution. (Here the criterion is the acceptance of an application rather than a definite date of admission. The latter is usually not possible to obtain from any institution.)

4. For the terminal care of an elderly person who himself (as well as his family) prefers to remain at home rather than in a hospital.

5. Chronically ill elderly people, where it appears valid from a medical and casework standpoint to provide this service. Frequently in such situations only part-time help may be needed. It brings relief to the family of the elderly person. In the course of the on-going process, it enables the family and the older person to mobilize themselves toward finding some other solution. The agency sees a valid function even in the relief this help brings while the service is given.

145

In all of these situations, the role of the FA is to assist the housewife or other responsible adults in the family with the management of the house. The FA is allowed to do the following household tasks: cooking for the primary family (older person and adult, non-married children living in the home), shopping, cleaning (no scrubbing or window washing), personal laundry.

The FA is definitely not used as a substitute domestic, neither does she take the place of a practical nurse. The service is really designed to take over the job any housewife would be doing during a crisis in her family, if she were well. It is geared toward making the elderly person more comfortable, physically and emotionally.

Family Aides are trained to do simple home nursing: take temperatures, give sponge baths, even assist a handicapped person with a regular bath, use bed pans, give prescribed medication, change bed linens without removing the patient from bed (no injections or dressings), etc.

Our FA's are particularly trained to know the limit of the agency's responsibility in relation to a sick person. Therefore, they are allowed to use their own judgment to call a doctor or a relative if they sense or observe a change in the client's condition. Generally, our experience has shown that the FA is called upon to use her own judgment on many occasions. This work calls for well integrated, stable women who can apply the limits set by the agency and still remain flexible and patient.

Since part-time FA help has proven so helpful, our FA's frequently carry two assignments simultaneously. This requires of the FA recognition of the need for individualization as well as very basic personal organization.

FULL-TIME LIMIT IN FAMILY AIDE SERVICE

The beginning time limit for FA service, whether given on a full-time basis (45 hours a week) or part-time, is one month.

If the ongoing process reveals that the service is well used and meets the need of the particular situation, it may be extended to *three months*. This usually requires reevaluation of the medical picture, and in cases where another community agency is involved, such as a home for aged, hospital, or other institution, we also verify the status of the application with the particular community agency. The three months may be extended to *six months* for valid casework reasons. When an extension of time beyond the six months is required, administrative approval is required. In principle, FA service for older persons may be extended indefinitely where it proves important medically and emotionally. In several instances we have thus given this service for more than a year.

Inasmuch as a basic purpose of the FA service is to help the older person resume his responsibilities, it is always used with flexibility. For example, full-time service after a period may be tapered off to half time or to three days a week or to every other week, depending upon the requirements of the situation.

Acute illness usually requires full-time FA service. However, in Services for the Aged, we deal largely with people suffering from chronic conditions and their ability to organize their lives well is not improved as much by a great deal of help, as by *regular* and *consistent* assistance. Only the taking over of a few very basic necessary household chores by the FA may make it possible for the elderly housewife to continue to manage by herself. Usually the shopping, cooking and straightening out of the house enables the client to manage well for the rest of the day, provided these few basic chores have been attended to.

A factor much more characteristic for the older person than for the younger one, is the fact that the older person is left with few responsibilities in old age toward other people. It is difficult for him to mobilize himself around the "worth-whileness" of caring for himself. "Why should I cook for myself?" is a question very frequently encountered.

By the time the older person seeks outside help, he is worn out from the lack of a regular normal life, and it takes quite a while until the FA service brings him back to a normal state. If the service is used, this frequently happens, gradually a different pattern emerges. Part-time help also offers the unique psychological opportunity for the client to test his readiness to use himself and to mobilize his personal resources during the FA's absence. The FA, so to say, paves the way in this direction.

Part-time FA service has proven extremely helpful to married children who no longer want to carry full responsibility for their parents, but who at the same time are still able to do their share in line with their obligation.

Casework Procedures in the Use of Family Circle Service

All principles discussed previously in the sections on "Reception" and "Intake" apply here. In addition, however, eligibility is not completed until a *medical report* is obtained. Usually the primary client signs the authorization for medical information. If this is not possible, a responsible relative signs it.

Intake is usually not completed unless the older person himself consents to have the service.

It is the worker's responsibility to discuss in the application interview or at other points in the intake process, the following elements: time limit; specific responsibilities of the Family Aide; the fact that most of our Family Aides are Negroes; that they wear uniforms; FA lunch hours, etc. The agency's continuing interest is expressed in a regular contact with the client, his family, and when indicated, medical verification and financial eligibility.

When the client expresses readiness to use the service and establishes his eligibility for it, the caseworker notifies the Supervisor and the Family Aide is selected and assigned for the particular situation.

The caseworker confers with Family Aide in a specially arranged appointment for this purpose. The agency does not require that the FA know what financial arrangements have been made by the family with the worker.

The Family Aide is introduced to the family by the caseworker in a previously arranged home appointment. This first joint interview with the FA is for the purpose of reviewing all conditions, hours, tasks, and if the FA does not remain in the home for the same day, a definite date for regular interviews with the caseworker are scheduled within her working hours. So then she may have to take time out for the purpose of keeping the appointment. On part-time assignments, this is not necessary, as the FA can find time outside of the job.

The continued casework process takes place in accordance with all the principles outlined earlier in the section on "Ongoing" process.

Occasionally during the ongoing process joint interviews with client, FA, and worker are arranged. This usually happens when some change is planned in relation to hours, responsibilities, etc.

The agency sometimes allows for change of FA's when a distinct clash of personalities occur. This, however, calls for a very careful evaluation of the relationship and the use the client tends to make of the service. Changes of FA's may also be made, particularly in long time situations, where the burden carried by the FA is considered to be too difficult.

In this service, home interviews take place more frequently than in other services, yet whenever the physical condition warrants it, office interviews are arranged.

APPENDIX C

PRIVATE RESIDENCE PROGRAM

(from "Casework Process in a Private Residence Program for Older Persons," *Journal of Social Work Process* 4, May 1953)

I should like to turn now to a more specific discussion of private residence placement for older persons and its implications for client and agency. This type of service has been called by different names—foster home plan, boarding home service, etc. Our own preference in the Jewish Community Services of Long Island has been to call it a Private Residence Program and this is the term that will be used throughout.

Private residence placement for the aged is a relatively new departure in the care of older persons unable to live in their own homes. Until very recently the only community facility available for the comparatively well aged person in need of substitute home care was the institution for the aged. In recent years, however, as a result of the increasing numbers of older persons in the general population as well as in the numbers requiring care, serious question has arisen as to whether the institution must continue to be the only major resource for care of aged persons. In addition to the practical question of how far institutions can expand, there have arisen psychological questions as to the validity of institutional care for all who cannot live in their own homes. Likewise, cognizance has been taken of the fact that many, if not most, older persons do not select institutional care as a first choice when they come to the point of needing substitute care. As a result of these and many other factors social agencies dealing with older persons, as well as social planning groups, have considered the possibility of other types of program for older persons.

In considering various types of non-institutional care, agencies have taken a page out of the child care book, and much of the current thinking on the care of the aged is not unlike that which was done in the children's field.

In terms of services this division makes available to persons over 60 all the regular agency-wide services such as psychiatric diagnosis and treatment, family aide (homemaker) service, adult child-parent counseling and other similar services. In addition, however, this division makes available special services not available in the other agency divisions. These include referrals to homes for the aged, nursing homes, and the Private Residence Program.

I should like to describe briefly the general characteristics of the Private Residence Program as it operates in the Jewish Community Services. The Program involves the placement of persons aged 60 and over with private families. In carrying out this service the agency has set up requirements, policies and procedures for both client and private residence owner.

CLIENT

Eligibility for this service is limited to Jewish persons in the Greater New York area, aged 60 and over. Occasionally the service is made available to persons under the age of 60 where for casework reasons this appears indicated. The second basic eligibility requirement is the inability of the older person to live either with his adult children or by himself as the result of emotional or physical difficulties or both. The physical or medical requirements are very flexible. Only those persons who are completely bedridden are considered ineligible. All other persons even those partially ambulatory and in need of special care are considered physically eligible. Similarly eligible are persons with a background of mental illness. Actually then, from a physical or medical standpoint the program excludes only those requiring custodial care. More important as far as we are concerned is the emotional readiness on the part of the older client to become involved in a casework process with the agency around his request for placement and the acceptance of the various requirements of the placement process.

Another requirement is to undergo a complete medical examination by the agency physician at some point prior to placement. The purpose of this is less to determine eligibility for placement than to ascertain correctly the state of the client's current condition in order to know precisely the type of care to be required once in placement. In all instances it is the worker and the agency who determine final eligibility for placement.

A final requirement is a financial one—the ability to reimburse the agency a minimum sum of $70 per month. This amount was chosen because it is the equivalent of what the Department of Welfare pays to Old Age Assistance clients living in boarding homes. The thought of the agency was that any older person unable to pay this minimum sum might be eligible for Old Age Assistance. Exceptions to this rule are made where clients unable to pay this amount are found by the Department of Welfare to be ineligible for assistance. In these instances lower payments are mutually arrived at. Where, on the basis of our fee scale, larger payments can be made, this is worked out in detail. The maximum payment is $130 per month which is the sum paid to residence owners for each client.

In accepting the client for placement the agency commits itself to permanent care. In the event the client is unable to continue in placement, help is given in leading him to other facilities. In placement the agency provides medical care by its own physicians, clothing and other budgetary needs where necessary, as well as referrals to employment and recreation facilities.

ment as a move towards the reestablishment of long lost independence and security. For in living with their children they had experienced a striking reversal of roles. It was their children who took care of them, who supplied them with daily necessities, who supplied them with money and clothing and food. They had lost their traditional parental role to their children. The inability any longer to live with their children is in most instances a result of this struggle for reassertion of role and for independence. To the adult children in this type of situation, request for the placement of a parent becomes an assertion for freedom from an unnatural role of super-parent although it is seldom presented in this way because of feelings of guilt.

To the older person who does not live with his children but who has maintained his own living independence, application for placement will more nearly emphasize feelings of dependence and futility. Usually, the request for placement is made at the point where the client begins to feel physically unable to take care of all of his personal needs. A heart condition, for instance, may make it inadvisable for him to go out for his meals three times a day, or a chronic illness of another type may require the need of frequent attention he is unable to secure in his furnished room or apartment.

To this person, coming to the agency for help in placement will precipitate considerable struggle in an effort to hold on to as much independence as possible. The ambivalent feelings of not wanting to give up what he has, and yet having to face the reality of a change, will usually bring forth an expression of distrust, centered on procedures or on the whole placement function. The client may, for example, raise questions about the need for income verification or an examination by our doctor. He may also question whether we actually have homes that will consider such a person as he is, and if we do have such homes "they are probably doing it for the money anyhow."

In both types of situations the reality of the request for

placement—private residence placement—which permits the
client to remain in the community as long as possible affords
the agency and worker a real opportunity for giving constructive casework help. For one thing, the very nature of
the service which emphasizes living in the community as
against institutional placement, which, in people's minds is
synonymous with dependence, enables the worker to help
the client face realistically the degree of help he actually
needs. Essentially, this type of placement has been made
available only to those who can utilize their strengths in it.
We do not require as a condition of placement the client's
total subservience to agency or home. We do not control
his coming or going nor do we require him, as a condition
of placement, to give up his friends, or treasured possessions
which he may want to bring with him into the home. Similarly beyond the initial and continued vertification of income
the agency does not require the client to "sign over" everything to the agency, and by the same token the client has
the choice of either remaining in placement or leaving it if
it does not meet his requirements.

From the very beginning of the client's coming the
agency accepts and is ready to recognize his cultural and
religious background. It has not been proven by our experience that older persons are more interested in religion
than younger people are. What we have seen is an intensification of previous attitudes and practices, perhaps in the
same degree that the need for security emphasizes a desire
to hold on to money or possessions. To the degree that such
attitudes and feelings enable the client to live securely they
are encouraged.

One of the important lessons we have learned in working
with older people is that all of these factors—which may
hold for all persons—manifest themselves in an exaggerated
form. Attitudes towards money, for example, the need of
an older person who no longer feels accepted in the labor
market to have a reserve come through more sharply than
in casework with younger persons. This is true for accept-

ance of change generally. In work with older persons allowance must be made for greater struggle, for a greater "time" factor and for special differences which assume reality for them. In this latter category, I would put as valid a concern, for example, with death and funeral arrangements. One must be aware also of what might be termed the "classic" content of an older person's speech, reverting to the past; the need to tell of his importance and influence in his younger years; the implications of doubt in the "young" worker's ability to understand him. All of these are special factors, which we must accept as valid for the older person.

THE PLACEMENT PROCESS

We have found it helpful both for client and agency to think of placement as having three separate phases—pre-placement, residence placement, and end-of-placement. Each of these phases is, of course, interrelated with each other. Yet, each is viewed as having a structure and focus of its own based upon the nature of the phase and its meaning both for client and agency. I should like now to discuss each of these phases and to cite a few case illustrations.

A. *The Pre-Placement Phase*

The pre-placement phase may be broadly defined as the period from the client's initial contact with the agency up to the point where he actually moves into the private residence. In considering how this very crucial phase can be made more meaningful to clients and more focused, we have sub-divided this phase further into several steps which I shall now describe:

1. *Reception.* This is defined as the initial contact which the client or his family has with agency. It may be a telephone call or a letter requesting service. In our agency such a call involving an older person is immediately transferred to the caseworker of the Division on Services for Aged. (This is a general agency policy. The telephone operator

merely ascertains whether the problem is with a child, family or older person, and immediately transfers the call to the worker in the appropriate division.) The caseworker in this initial discussion will determine gross eligibility factors such as proper residence, age, etc. If eligible, in this regard, an appointment will be offered. If it is an adult child or relative who phones we make it clear that we would have to see the older person, although we stand ready to see the adult child or relative in a first appointment if that is his wish.

2. *Intake.* The first appointment is considered the beginning of the intake process. The total process may involve as many appointments with the older client and his children as are necessary to determine whether private residence placement is what he wants, whether he is eligible from the agency standpoint, emotional stability, physical condition, financial requirements and other arrangements.

Part of the intake process, although usually coming as the final aspect of it, is the physical examination by the agency physician. The purpose of this examination is to know, medically, the older client, his need for special diets, care, etc., rather than as a determination of eligibility for placement. The final determination in each instance, as indicated earlier, rests with agency and worker.

3. *Residence selection.* Having determined eligibility the worker goes about selecting a suitable home for the client. The list of homes, vacancies, characteristics and description of homes is centrally administered. The worker in need of a home fills in a form which goes to the worker in charge of this file. Appropriate referrals are made after which the client's worker reads the records and confers with the worker of the residence. On the basis of the decision of both workers the residence owner is contacted first by her own worker, then by the worker of the client. The discussion with the residence owner is on a very tentative basis, allowing both worker and residence owner to react to each other as well as to the client pending placement. It will be

and all encompassing way. Stating this in its simplest form we do not expect a client to be able to develop a relationship to his worker or to be able to recognize his feelings in coming to an agency for help in, let us say, one interview. To expect this would be to expect the client to master the totality of this new and often fearful situation. To help a client relate to his request for service, and to recognize his feelings, it is necessary to break up the totality as it were or to "partialize" the elements that go into the request for help. This partialization, of course, must stem from the agency as part of the casework process in any given situation. We cannot prevent clients from total reactions, but we can, at least through the process of partialization, help them to react less totally to the service given them.

It is this important element which has impelled us to set up the trial period of placement. I need not repeat here the fear and anxiety that older persons have in requesting placement. This has been covered before. There is no less fear— even though the client has gone through the pre-placement phase—in approaching actual placement. To the client actual placement, the final act of separation from his previous surroundings into a new and unknown situation, creates new fears, doubts and questions. Will he really be able to get along with his new hosts; will he like the food, his new bed; will his hosts really care?

In recognizing the reality of these feelings we have also recognized that many of them, or at least their intensity, stem from the attitude or notion that the placement will have to be a permanent one. The "forever" quality of a placement, or the feeling of having to make an immediate adjustment we have found thus makes for an intensification of the normal fears that any change involves. Our thought in setting up a three-month trial period aims at eliminating the need for feeling that adjustment must be immediate, that the placement once made can never be terminated without opportunity for another home.

Both client and residence owner are made aware that the

three-month trial period is a testing out period for both. There will be complaints, negative reactions, arguments about food, heat, light, sleeping arrangements, etc. During this period, the caseworker is likewise involved with the clients on a weekly basis in order to help both relate to each other. Part of the arrangement is that both client and residence owner will allow each other at least this much time, despite difficulties that may arise and which at another point in the permanent phase would result in a request for replacement.

The trial period is not used rigidly and the choice of a three-month period rather than a lesser or longer time is based upon our experience in viewing an older person's adjustment time. Certainly an obviously difficult situation would not require client, residence owner or agency to stick it out to the limit. On the other hand, even in such a situation requiring an earlier change there is an absence of immediate pressure, because of the arrangement. In an obviously positive situation we would also introduce gradual changes such as a tapering off of the worker's weekly contacts although we would be inclined to hold to the three-month period as still valid by utilizing it as the beginning period of placement.

I hope I have not implied that all problems of adjustment are worked out in the first three months. What has been implied is that there is great need for allowing sufficient time, with as little pressure as possible to enable the older client to make his beginning adjustment to a new separation experience.

As the end of the three-month trial period is approached, the worker usually has a joint interview with both client and residence owner. The worker also makes it a point to see the adult children at such a time as well. The past period is reviewed and discussed with a view to pointing up those elements on which stress will have to be put in the future.

2. *The Permanent Residence Period.* This might be called the ongoing period of placement. The client and

residence owner have by this time made a beginning adjustment to each other. There has been established an understanding of each other's habits and ways, and the agency,
too, has defined for them and for itself its role in the situation.

The permanent placement period lasts for as long as the
client remains in placement or until it is terminated either
by death or some plan decided upon mutually. We shall
discuss later the ending period of placement in instances
where there can be a planned ending. For our present purpose, however, the permanent period is to be seen as one
which generally lacks any stated ending in terms of time.

The content for the worker during this period ranges
over the whole gamut of every-day living for the client and
homeowner: helping the client in meeting agency requirements of financial payment, relationship to adult children
and other members of his family, help in receiving adequate
medical and dental care, help in finding employment or
participating in recreational and educational activities. In
addition there are the many new problems which come up
as the client continues in placement. The major emphasis
in the ongoing period is to help the client use himself as
creatively as possible within the limits of his physical and
mental capacities. Within this framework there is always
a continuing evaluation of the client's desire for placement
and his ability to use the service. During this period there
is a further clarification of role with the client's adult children in terms of their attitudes toward placement and their
responsibilities toward the parent, whether it be financial or
of another type.

C. *The Ending Phase*

The agency, in accepting older persons for private residence placement does so with the understanding that the
client may remain in placement permanently. At no time,
however, is it implied that the decision to enter placement

is irrevocable. Both client and agency are free to terminate placement where continuation of the service can no longer be of help to client, or where the agency can no longer fulfill its purpose of helping the client to remain in the community.

Similarly, unlike other types of placement—that of children or young adults—one cannot consider as a major goal of placement the ultimate discharge of the client. The physical and psychological reasons necessitating the placement of aged persons make such a goal in a universal sense completely impractical. On the other hand, discharge does become a legitimate factor for consideration where the client after a period of placement is unable to adjust to living with a family or where the client deteriorates so physically and mentally that he is unable to use the dynamics of placement. In such instances where termination of placement becomes a necessary agency, client, and his family do become involved in an ending process.

In addition to the types of ending mentioned above there is one type of situation which lends itself particularly to a dynamic process. This is the situation where a client requests placement only for a definite period of time, or for an interim period pending admission to an institution. Although in the latter instance the specific ending date may not be known it is nevertheless possible to become engaged around ending with him.

In ending placement the client presents attitudes and feelings that are strikingly similar to those that he presents in beginning placement. He has the same fears and doubts in leaving what is known and going into the unknown. And unless the client decides to return to his former habitat which is a known element to him and hence holds less fear, he will approach ending with considerable trepidation. This is particularly true for clients who have reached their turn on waiting lists of homes for the aged. It is with this group of clients that we have had most of our experience in endings. Although there is usually an expression of satisfaction that they have finally been called, doubts are raised about it. There is awareness that institutional life will be different, that they will have to adjust to group living. There is fear about having to share a room with many people and there is insecurity about having to adhere to routines of coming and going. The client will often express considerable guilt over the "troubles" of agency and residence owner in helping him adjust to the residence and will often vacillate in his thoughts on whether actually to go into the institution.

The attitudes of the worker and his part in helping the client during this period are extremely important. For while the worker cannot help but be aware of the differences between institutional and private residence placement, it is the client who in the last analysis must take responsibility for his decision.

CONCLUSION

In concluding this discussion of the casework process in a private residence program for older persons I must point out that I have limited myself to only several aspects of the program. I have not touched upon the whole area of residence-finding as a casework process or on work with residence owners, both of which are large subjects unto themselves and which will eventually have to be written about in order to understand the program more completely. Nor have I discussed the continuing work with adult children during the period of placement of the parent. This, too, is an area that requires presentation.

APPENDIX D

A Chronological Bibliography of the Publications
and Papers of William Posner

"A Re-Evaluation of Foster Home Care." *Jewish Social Service Quarterly* XVI (September 1939), pp. 92–98.

"Aspects of Process in Student Supervision." *Social Work Today* (December 1941).

"The Use of Structure in Homefinding." In "Three Papers on Homefinding." Publication of the New York Association for Jewish Children Foster Home Bureau, April 30, 1943, pp. 16–26.

"An Experiment in Homefinding Promotion." *Jewish Social Service Quarterly* XX (June 1944), pp. 216–18.

"Jewish Education in a Foster Home Agency." *Jewish Social Service Quarterly* XXIII (March 1947), pp. 304–5.

"Jewish Content in Child Placement." *Jewish Social Service Quarterly* XXIV (March 1948), pp. 268–73.

"Discussion on Paper Presented by Central Bureau for Jewish Aged." Institute on Jewish Component in Casework, April 12, 1949.

"A Private Residence Program for Older Persons." Presented at a panel discussion on "New Trends in Care of the Aged." National Conference of Jewish Social Welfare, Cleveland, June 10, 1949. Also in "Council Reports." Council of Jewish Federation and Welfare Funds, New York.

"New York City's Work with the Elderly." Presented at Public Hearing, Joint Legislative Committee on Problems of the Aging, December 8, 1949. Also in *Young at any Age*. Published by the New York State Joint Legislative Committee on Problems of the Aging, Legislative Document #12, 1950, pp. 68–71.

Posner and Hofstein, Saul, "The Use of the Agency's Jewishness in Casework Process." *Social Service Quarterly* XXVI (March 1950), pp. 332–40.

"The Problems of the Aging in a Changing Society." Remarks at Fall Conference of Queensboro Council for Social Welfare, October 19, 1950.

Posner and Galpern, M., "Intake Process in Homes for the Aged." Presented at the National Conference on Jewish Social Welfare, 1950. Also in *Administration of Homes for the Aged*. Council of Jewish Federation and Welfare Funds, New York, 1951, pp. 92–94.

"A Private Family Agency Sets up a Special Unit for the Aged." Presented at the New York State Welfare Conference, Buffalo, November 13, 1951.

"Casework Process in a Private Residence Program for Older Persons." December 1951. Published in *Journal of Social Work Process* 4, (May 1953), pp. 9–28, and by National Social Welfare Assembly under title, "A Foster Home Program for Older Persons," November 1952.

"Manual of Policies and Procedures for Passover Assistance Program." Prepared for the Jewish Community Services of Long Island, March 4, 1952.

"Developments in Casework and Counseling Services for the Aged in New York City, 1940–1950." Presented at the Annual Meeting and Conference of the Welfare and Health Council of New York City, April 29, 1952.

"Casework with the Aged as a Specialized Service in a Multiple Service Agency." In "Professional Implications of Multiple Service." Three Papers presented in Celebration of the 10th Anniversary of the Jewish Community Services of Long Island, October 1952.

Posner and Miller, Lurie A., "Cooperation between Mental Hospital and Social Agency in Providing Private Residence Care for Voluntary Mental Patients." *Journal of the Hillside Hospital* II, no. 1 (January 1953), pp. 36–40. Also as paper titled "Private Residence Care in an Urban Environment for Discharged Patients from a Voluntary Private Mental Hospital."

"Meeting the Needs of the Aged in the Community." Presented at the Annual Conference, Central Atlantic Region of the Council of Jewish Federations and Welfare Funds, Atlantic City, March 8, 1953.

"A Dynamic Casework Philosophy and Program in Work with the Aged." *The Councilor* (Baltimore Council of Social Agencies) XVIII (September 1953), pp. 25–36.

"The Merits of a Counseling Service in a Community Centered Agency." National Social Welfare Assembly, January 1954. Mimeographed.

Posner and Farber, Arthur S., "Mrs. Benson Requests Placement." In *The Field of Social Work*. Edited by Arthur E. Fink, Everett E. Wilson, Merrill B. Conover. New York: Henry Holt & Co., 1955, pp. 477–99.

"New Horizons in Casework with the Aged." Presented at the Institute New Horizons for Casework with the Aged, New York, March 31, 1955, Welfare and Health Council of New York City. Prepared by Posner but representing the combined thinking of the Study Group on Casework with the Aged of the Division on Welfare of Aged of the Welfare and Health Council.

"The Role of the Family Agency in Strengthening Family Life." Presented at Jewish Social Service, Hartford, April 21, 1955.

"Outline of Rochester Speech." June 5, 1955.

"The Family Agency and Chronic Illness." *The Jewish Chronically Ill—A Community Responsibility*, Council of Jewish Federation and Welfare Funds, New York, 1955.

"Developing New Attitudes toward the Old." *The Jewish Parent* (March 1956), pp. 14–16.

Posner and Indelman, Rochelle, "Jewish Community Services of Long Island—Manual of Policies and Procedures in the Division of Services for the Aged." March 1956. Mimeographed.

Posner and Lurie, A.; Miller, A. S.; Pinsky, L.; and Vogelstein, H., "The Placement of Discharged Mental Patients in Foster Homes: A Cooperative Project between Mental Hospital and Family Agency." 1955 Milton Weill Annual Award, Federation of Jewish Philanthropies, New York. Also in *Journal of the Hillside Hospital* V, no. 34 (October 1956).

"Adapting and Sharpening Social Work Knowledge and Skills in Serving the Aged." Presented at Metropolitan Washington Chapter of National Association of Social Workers, January 1957. Published in *Social Work* 2 no. 4 (October 1957), pp. 37–42.

"Adapting Family Agency Philosophy and Programs to Serve the Aged." Presented at the National Conference on Social Welfare, Philadelphia, May 22, 1957. Also titled "The Challenge of Specialization in Family Agency Services for the Aged." Mimeographed.

"Casework with the Aged: Challenge or Retreat." *American Journal of Orthopsychiatry* XXVIII, no. 2 (April 1958), pp. 328–33.

"Socio-Cultural Factors in Casework with Adult Children and Aged Parents." Presented at National Conference of Jewish Communal Service, Chicago. May 19, 1958. Published in *Journal of Jewish Communal Service* XXXV, no. 2 (Winter 1958), pp. 193–201.

"A Case History of the Development of Non-Institutional Services for the Aged." Presented at the Annual Meeting of the Florida Council on Aging, Tampa, May 22, 1958.

"Casework with the Aged: Developments and Trends." Position Paper on Casework prepared for the Aspen Seminar Council on Social Work Education, Aspen, Colorado, September 1958. Condensed version published in *Social Work Education for Better Social Services to the Aging* II, Council on Social Work Education, New York, 1959, pp. 1–14.

"The Family Agency's Responsibility to the Families of Aged Clients." *Social Casework* XXXIX (November 1958), pp. 512–16.

"Programming for the Three Generation Family." Remarks at National Jewish Welfare Board, Consultation on Family Programming, December 1958.

"Fulfilling Homemaking and Housekeeping Needs." Pittsburgh Bicentennial, University of Pittsburgh, May 27, 1959.

"The Role and Opportunity of National Organizations in Improving Services to Aging Individuals." Paper for the National Committee on the Aging, New York, May 1959.

"Summary of Spring Workshop." Nassau County Council of Social Agencies, Adelphi College, May 1959.

"New Solutions to Age-Old Problems." Nassau County Council of Social Agencies, Adelphi College, May 25, 1959.

"Retrospect and Prospect in Casework with the Aged." Presented at the Annual Meeting of National Conference of Jewish Communal Service, Pittsburgh, June 2, 1959. Published in *Journal of Jewish Communal Service* XXXVI (Winter 1959), pp. 120–29.

"The Specifics of Casework Process with the Older Client." Massachusetts State Conference of Social Work, Boston, November 7, 1959.

"Jewish Content in Social Work Process." Assembly Commission on Synagogue Relations, Federation of Jewish Philanthropies, New York City, December 21, 1959. Published by Federation of Jewish Philanthropies, vol. 2, no. 8, February–March 1960, pp. 21–23.

"Older Years, Enriching Years." *Journal of the Long Island Consultation Center* (January 1960), pp. 6–8.

"The Essential Character of a Foster Home Program for Older Persons." Seminar on Housing, National Committee on the Aging, Lake Mohawk, New York, June 15, 1960.

"Characteristics of Casework with Older People—A Discussion of Basic Issues, Seminar on Casework with Older People, The National Committee on the Aging, Arden House, Harriman, New York, October 31, 1960. Condensed version published as "Basic Issues in Casework with Older People," *Social Casework* XLIII, no. 5–6, May–June 1961, pp. 234–40.

"Analysis of the New York State Recommendations for the 1961 White House Conference." Prepared for New York State Welfare Conference, New York City, November 1960.

"The Effect of Changing Social Need on Interagency and Community Relations." (Discussion), *Journal of Social Work Process* 11 (1960), pp. 53–57.

"Aging with a Future." *Jewish Life* (April 1961), pp. 17–22.

"Jewishness as an Issue in Jewish Social Work." Written circa 1958. Published in *The Jewish Social Work* 2, no. 2 (Spring 1965).

INDEX

Acceptance, 22, 24, 68, 110

Action, 22, 24, 68--94, 95-109

Administration on Aging, 11

Adult children, 53-54, 77, 155, 163 (*see also* Generational component)

Affirmation of difference, 7, 57-58, 63-64, 87, 130-31

Agencies, 34, 51, 61, 68-94, 101, 126-37

Aging, development, 25, 116-17, 139-40

    fulfillment, 18, 25, 105, 124-25, 139, 142

    process, 40, 114-117, 140

    stereotype of, 24-25, 27, 36

American Geriatrics Association, 106

Aptekar, Herbert H., 20-21, 58-59

Attitudes, 17, 21-22, 24-37, 43, 66, 141

Bardwell, Francis, 103

Beatty, David J., 13

Benjamin Rose Institute of Cleveland, 9

Billingsley, Andrew, 7

Birren, James, 9

Blenkner, Margaret, 7, 11, 59

Brecher, Ruth and Edward, 10

Briar, Scott, 8, 12

Brodsky, Rose, 19

Brody, Elaine, 11

Browning, Grace, 41, 104

Business counseling and loans, 85-86

Busse, Ewald, 9

Casework (*see* social work)

Center for the Study of Aging and Human Development, Duke University, 9

Change, 47-48, 111, 130 (*see also* Growth)

Chen, Yung-Ping, 12

Chicago Conference on Care of the Aged, 103

Client-centered service, 71, 75, 79, 82

Cohen, Nathan, 111

Communication, 51, 118

Community living, 6-7, 73-75, 120, 150

Concentration, 8 (*see also* Specialization)

Continuity, 50, 73

Council on Social Work Education, 8

    Aspen Conference, 4, 11, 102-107

    Allerton House Conference, 11

Culture, 7, 50, 61-62, 126-137 (*see also* Socio-cultural factor)

Death, 9-10, 31, 33, 36, 43-44, 66

Dependence, 51-55, 65, 116, 154-55

Depression, 50-51

Dignity and worth, 17, 49-50, 97, 124-25, 133, 135

Donahue, Wilma, 9

Education, on aging, 114-117, 123, 140

    social work, 10-11, 106, 113-115

Employment counseling, 83-84

Encyclopedia of Social Work, 5

Ethnic identity, 130-31

Family, (periodical) 104

Family aide service, 78-81, 145-149

Family relations, 11, 57, 61, 70, 80-81, 101, 117, 130

Family Service Association Project on Aging, 10-11

172